THE TRADITIONS COMMON TO THE GOSPELS OF LUKE AND JOHN

SUPPLEMENTS

TO

NOVUM TESTAMENTUM

VOLUME VII

LEIDEN
E. J. BRILL
1963

THE TRADITIONS COMMON TO THE GOSPELS OF LUKE AND JOHN

by

JOHN AMEDEE BAILEY

LEIDEN
E. J. BRILL
1963

PRINTED IN THE NETHERLANDS

TABLE OF CONTENTS

INTRODUCTION

Since the finding of the first of the scrolls at Qumran in 1947, the discovery that elements in various documents of the Dead Sea covenanters are similar to material in the gospel of John has strengthened the position of those who stress the existence of much genuinely Palestinian material in the fourth gospel. [1] The effect of this has been to raise once again the old question as to whether John's gospel may not in fact be earlier than, and therefore independent of, the synoptic gospels. The present writer believes that an analysis of the material of Luke's and John's gospels at the points (occurring above all in their accounts of the events of the passion and the events following the resurrection) at which the two gospels agree with each other but depart from Mark and Matthew shows that John in at least some of these places was dependent on Luke's gospel in its present form. The present monograph consists of such an analysis, and in the writer's opinion proves that John, though his gospel unquestionably contains much genuinely Palestinian material, did draw on Luke and therefore cannot have written his gospel earlier than the eighties of the first century AD.

The subject of the Lucan-Johannine parallels has once before been extensively examined, by Julius Schniewind in his monograph *Die Parallelperikopen bei Lukas und Johannes* (1914). Schniewind maintained that John did not know Luke's gospel, and that another explanation for all the agreements must be found. It is the view of the writer that Schniewind was mistaken on this point, though indeed John's knowledge of Luke by no means explains all the points of similarity, as we shall see. The scope of the present work is somewhat larger than Schniewind's, in that it is not limited to an analysis of the passages where some verbal similarity evinces itself, but deals also with the two gospels at points where they contain related elements which, while not verbally similar, yet raise historical questions concerning the events of Jesus' life, e.g. the Last Discourses, and Jesus' activity in Samaria. However, no

---

[1] See e. g. Albright, "Recent Discoveries in Palestine and the Gospel of John," *The Background of the New Testament and its Eschatology*, ed. W. D. Davies and D. Daube, and Mowry, "The Dead Sea Scrolls and the Background for the Gospel of John," *The Biblical Archaeologist*, 1954.

purely theological similarities, such as those which exist, for example, between the doctrines of the Spirit of the two gospels, have been treated (though they have occasionally been mentioned), as that would have resulted in a work which, in view of the degree of scholarship required for a doctoral dissertation, would have been too long; the similarities—and dissimilarities—between the theologies of the two evangelists constitute, nevertheless, an exceedingly interesting subject, and one which it is the writer's hope that he can treat later in a companion piece to the present study.

The present study was written under the direction of Prof. Oscar Cullmann, to whom the writer wishes to take this opportunity to express his thanks.

November 1962

St. Paul's United Theological College, Limuru, Kenya

CHAPTER ONE

THE ANOINTING OF JESUS AND THE MARY-MARTHA STORIES

Luke 7. 36-50 / John 12. 1-8

Both Luke (7. 36-50) and John (12. 1-8) contain accounts of the anointing of Jesus' feet by a woman, accounts containing one striking parallel: in both the woman dries his feet with her hair. [1] Moreover in John's account the woman's name is Mary, and Martha, identified in Jn. 11. 1 as her sister, is mentioned as serving—all of which is reminiscent of Lk. 10. 38 ff., where sisters with the same names dominate an incident in which Jesus is, as in Jn. 12. 1 ff., a guest, and where Martha also (v. 10) serves. Though these are not the first parallels which occur in the two gospels, we shall examine them first because they demonstrate the fact that John knew Luke's gospel.

Is there evidence that the author of one of these accounts has drawn on the other? In themselves the verbal similarities (Lk.: ταῖς θριξὶν τῆς κεφαλῆς αὐτῆς ἐξέμασσεν, Jn: ἐξέμαξεν ταῖς θριξὶν αὐτῆς) do not ensure this, for the same action could hardly be otherwise described. [2] Moreover, the contexts in which these words are found differ significantly. In Luke the anointing occurs in the house of Simon a Pharisee who has invited Jesus there as his guest, [3] the woman is a prostitute the sign of whose repentence is that she bathes Jesus' feet in her tears, wipes the feet with her hair, and kisses and anoints them. The anointing is integrally related [4] to a

---

[1] It may be assumed in the course of this monograph that the statement is made that a feature is common to Luke and John only when this feature is found neither in Mark nor Matthew—unless, of course, the opposite is explicitly stated.

[2] So, correctly, Schniewind, *op. cit.*, p. 23.

[3] Where the incident takes place isn't clear. The position in the gospel points to Galilee, but as Bernard, *Gospel according to St. John*, p. 410, says, v. 34 makes it likely that the incident's being narrated at this point is due solely to thematic considerations.

[4] The passage is not free of difficulties, which have given rise to a number of surgical efforts, for which see the commentaries. We need not discuss them there. Suffice it to say that the vivid picture of the sinner's weeping and anointing action does not, as Bultmann, *Geschichte der synoptischen*

short discourse by Jesus highlighted by a parable, the occasion of which is Simon's reproach of Jesus. In John, on the other hand, the incident occurs in Bethany at the opening of the events of the final Passover, in the presence of Lazarus, with Mary anointing Jesus' feet. But here, what she wipes from his feet with her hair is not as in Luke her tears, but the ointment; and the incident results in Jesus' defending her action against Judas Iscariot, who has complained of the waste of the expensive ointment. In contrast to these sharp divergences are the extraordinary contacts between John's account and that contained in Mk. 14. 3-9 (which Matthew follows closely): (a) the 300 *denarii* as the price of the ointment, (b) the location of the incident in Bethany, at the beginning of the passion account, (c) the reproach to Jesus about the woman's extravagance, (d) Jesus' statement about the poor made in defense of the woman, (e) the reference to the anointing of Jesus' body after his death, above all (f) the occurrence of πιστικός, a word of uncertain meaning found nowhere else in Greek literature as early as this its sole use in the New Testament. [1] These similarities, especially the use of πιστικός, make it absolutely certain that John has here drawn on Mark, using Mark's text directly as a source, and that he means to record the same event as Mark does.

But John has not only drawn heavily on Mark, he has taken two elements, the anointing of the feet and the drying with hair, from Luke's account. The latter detail fits very badly in John's account [2]; it is inexplicable that the salve would be wiped off by Mary—the whole point is that it should remain on the feet. The fact that a very large amount of salve [3] was used cannot by

Tradition, pp. 19 f. maintains, give the impression of having been composed by the third evangelist on the basis of the very different anointing account in Mark and added to what Bultmann sees as the original element, the parable. Rather Luke replaces the Marcan anointing account by another one familiar to him. Plummer's exegesis, *Gospel according to St. Luke, ad loc.*, whereby the whole incident, with the possible exception of vv. 48-50, forms an integral whole, is more convincing; and indeed the Lucan account represents a tradition as independent of the Marcan tradition as it is (see below) of the Johannine.

[1] Matthew reads here instead of Mark's and John's νάρδου πιστκῆς simply βαρυτίμου.

[2] This, and the fact that the detail fits well in Luke, indicates that the borrowing was on John's part, not Luke's.

[3] A λίτρα if equivalent to the Latin pound (*libra*) is about 12 ounces (327. 45 grams), though Strack-Billerbeck, *Kommentar zum Neuen Testament aus Talmud und Midrasch*, II, *ad loc.*, according to rabbinic reckoning arrives at the somewhat smaller amount 273 gr.

itself be used to explain this action; indeed Jesus' statement in v. 7 can perhaps be used to support the view that only a part of the salve was used by the woman, but the meaning of this verse is not clear (Jesus does not say that Mary shall keep the *rest* of the salve for the day of his burial, but the salve itself: αὐτό), and v. 3b seems to oppose such an exegesis. Mary is not drawn as a repentant sinner in John's account, which rôle would explain the use of her hair instead of a towel. [1] One means of dealing with the difficulty is to eliminate the problematical words from John's text as late additions. So Bultmann tentatively [2] and Grant [3] definitely, on the basis of the slightly difficult repetition of τοὺς πόδας in v.3, and the fact that in a few unimportant manuscripts the words τοὺς πόδας αὐτοῦ precede instead of follow ταῖς θριξὶν αὐτῆς, label καὶ ἐξέμαξεν ταῖς θριξὶν αὐτῆς τοὺς πόδας αὐτοῦ as secondary, stemming from Luke. But the fact that all the manuscripts of any importance at all offer these words excludes this as a possibility.

The only explanation of these difficulties is that they stem from John's having purposely and carefully combined the accounts of the anointing as they appear in the present gospels of Mark and Luke, though the combination brought with it a striking unevenness. It is theoretically possible that the fourth evangelist isn't drawing on Luke at this point at all, but that these confusing words stem from his special, non-Marcan source, the source from which he also derived the information that the anointing took place six

[1] The fact that John does not also take over the tears and footkissing from Luke is probably to be explained on the basis of the fact that these two elements belong to Luke's portrait of the woman as a sinner; John, suppressing this identification, could not use them. To be sure, the drying with hair and probably the anointing of the feet in Luke belong also to the sinner motif; but John was able to use them without introducing the motif itself. It may, indeed, be that John used Luke from memory here, and only two of the most vivid details stuck in his mind. At any event, John did not see Mary as the sinner of Luke's account; he may not be cited, as Gardner-Smith, *St. John and the Synoptic Gospels*, p. 48, maintains he can, as supporting the Roman-Catholic theory (shared by Bernard, *op. cit.*, *ad loc.*) that the unnamed woman of Mark's account, Mary the sister of Martha, and Mary Magdalene (who is seen as the unnamed sinner of Luke's account as well as the anointer of John's, the latter being inferred from Jn 12. 7, though John does not mention the visit of Mary Magdalene to the tomb for the purpose of anointing Jesus' corpse, and in fact inserts an account of embalming by Joseph and Nichodemus which makes such a visit superfluous) are all one person.

[2] In *Das Evangelium des Johannes*, *ad loc.*

[3] Grant, "Was the Author of John dependent upon the Gospel of Luke?," *Journal of Biblical Literature* 1937, p. 290.

(according to modern means of reckoning, five) days before the Passover (not two, that is to say one, day before, as in Mark's account), the rôle of Mary (on Martha see below), and the rôle of Judas as a thief. [1] Such a thesis simplifies things, making John dependent on only two instead of three varying traditions, but it is not acceptable. The difficulties of John's account are explicable only on the basis of Mark's having been combined with Luke; if we assume these difficulties already existed in a source of his, we must also assume that that source knew, and combined, Mark and Luke—which is as unlikely as anything could be. No, the evidence here points clearly to John as having known the Lucan passage (and therefore Luke's gospel) in its present form. [2] What was John's

---

[1] There is no reason to imagine that John would have invented these details instead of taking them over from a written or oral source. Bultmann, indeed, *op. cit.*, *ad loc.*, points out that if John had invented these details, not Mary but Martha (as in ch. 11) would have played the main rôle in 12. 1-18; but Mary's rôle in ch. 11 is not so preponderant as to give this argument force.

[2] Schniewind, *op. cit.*, p. 24, maintains that the Luke 7 story was known to John, though not as part of Luke's gospel but "otherwise, from tradition or memory." But this vague suggestion gives rise to unnecessary circuitousness, and is unconvincing. In fact the Johannine anointing passages prove as clearly as such things can ever be proved that John knew Luke's gospel (as well as Mark's) in its present form—and we shall find this often confirmed in our examination of John, especially in his account of the passion. Therewith the view advanced by Zurhellen, *Die Heimat des vierten Evangeliums* (1909) (for those who before Zurhellen held this position see Schniewind, *op. cit.*, p. 2) in which he was followed by Schniewind, *op. cit.*, p. 95 and *passim*, Grant, *op. cit.*, pp. 303 f., Feine-Behm, *Einleitung in das Neue Testament*, p. 45, Gardner-Smith, *op. cit.*, pp. ix and 17, and Bultmann, "Zur johanneischen Tradition," *Theologische Literaturzeitung* 1955 columns 521-6, is proved to be mistaken. That is not to say that the view of H. J. Holtzmann ("Das schriftstellerische Verhältnis des Johannes zu den Synoptikern," *Zeitschrift für wissenschaftliche Theologie*, 1869, pp. 69-85, 448 f.) was right; he saw John as drawing everywhere on all three synoptic gospels, and attempted at all costs to derive everything in John, including his special material, from one of the other gospels; the result is that he underestimated the degree of John's departure from the others as well as John's theological creativity. John should not be understood as having constantly consulted the gospels of Mark and Luke as he wrote; his drawing on them can in most cases be explained on the basis of his drawing on his memory of them. Yet this explanation, as we have seen as regards his use of Mark's anointing passage, does not always suffice; moreover, he evinces, as we shall see, an extensive knowledge of Mark and Luke, of the kind which is not gathered from having read or heard them read once. That the two gospels in their finished form were accessible to him, to consult when he wished, is certain. Zurhellen's and Schniewind's view has therefore been correctly rejected by the great majority of critics, among whom may be named Schlatter (*Evangelium des*

reason for collating in a fashion not usual for him three literary traditions, or two literary and one oral tradition? Why does John follow so closely in the footsteps of the synoptic gospels here? The answer is that he is here approaching the account of Jesus' passion, and that he is, in this area of traditions unusually early crystallized, more dependent upon the synoptic gospels than is his wont earlier in the gospel.

One further element of John's account in 12. 1-8 is of importance to us: the presence in it (as in the account of the raising of Lazarus in ch. 11) of the sisters Mary and Martha. It is important to us because Luke (in 10. 38 ff.) adduces a story in which Martha and Mary also figure, and whose framework (Jesus as guest) is the same as in Jn. 12. 1 ff. And, though Mary in Lk. 10. 38 ff. and in Jn. 12. 1 ff. performs two quite different actions, Martha does the same thing in both—she serves. Furthermore, the note in John that Martha does so, contained in v. 2, is completely extrinsic, occurring in a story otherwise concerned only with Mary. Everything points to its being secondary, stemming from Lk. 10. 38 ff., and added by John on the basis of his knowledge of that passage in order to make it clear that the two women who figured in Jn. 11 and 12 were the same as those in Luke. Too much should not be made of this uncharacteristic action of John; he seldom writes his gospel, as he has done here, in such a way that it clearly supplements the synoptic tradition. He has done so here, probably from memory, [1] because, though he did not think Lk. 10. 38 ff. (unlike a number of the

Lukas, p. 465), Jülicher-Fascher (*Einleitung in das Neue Testament*, p. 384), H. Zimmermann ("Lukas und die johanneische Tradition," *Studien und Kritiken*, 1913, pp. 586-605), Windisch (*Johannes und die Synoptiker*, p. 43), Larfeld (*Die Neutestamentliche Evangelien*, pp. 351 ff.), Dibelius ("Johannesevangelium," *Die Religion in Geschichte und Gegenwart*, p. 353), Sigge (*Das Johannesevangelium und die Synoptiker*, p. 41), Gaussen ("The Lucan and the Johannine Writings," *Journal of Theological Studies*, 1908, pp. 563-8), Moffatt (*Introduction to the New Testament*, p. 535), Streeter (*The Four Gospels*, pp. 393 ff.), Barrett (*The Gospel according to St. John*, p. 14 and *passim*), Goguel (*Introduction au Nouveau Testament*, p. 222).

It is doubtful that John also knew Matthew's gospel; though at a number of points they are parallel where Mark and Luke differ from them (for a list of these see Zurhellen, *op. cit.*, p. 39, nt. 2, to which list the express designation of Judas as the traitor in Mt. 26. 25 and Jn. 13. 26 should be added), nevertheless John shows so little evidence of using Matthew that it is unlikely that he was acquainted with this gospel.

[1] That Mary, unlike her sister, served constitutes the root fact of the Lucan passage, and so is—as Mary's proverbial status ever since indicates—easily remembered.

elements of Luke's passion account, as we shall see) significant enough to include in his gospel, nevertheless he regarded the Lazarus story (which forms the climax of the first half of his gospel) and the anointing passage (which, as v. 7 makes clear, forms the introduction to the concluding half of his gospel) as so important that he wished to underline their relation to a tradition which he knew was, through Luke's gospel, already generally known in the Church.

As for the account of the raising of Lazarus in Jn. 11, [1] both Mary and Martha already figured in it when the story came into John's hands. It is evident that a cycle of traditions about the two sisters existed, one of which was incorporated by Luke into his gospel and another (that of the raising of Lazarus) by John into his. As for the anointing in John's gospel, as we have seen, the evangelist derived the information that the anointing woman was named Mary from a source, probably oral; there is no reason to think that this was a different Mary from the Mary of Lk. 7. 36 ff. and Jn. 11, i.e. that she was not the sister of Martha. The relationship was probably assumed in the oral source; John, however, incorporating it into his gospel, wrote it down in such a way as to make it clear that the Jn. 11 and 12 stories involved not only two women named Mary and Martha, but the two sisters of that name about whom at least one other story was generally known in the Church. [2] We are

---

[1] Zurhellen, *op. cit.*, p. 43, sees the mention of Mary in the ch. 11 story as secondary, basing this on the contention that her role there is insignificant, and attributing vv. 28-32, the main verses which deal with her, to the reviser whom he postulates for the gospel. His view is that the latter found only Martha named in the ch. 11 and only Mary named in the ch. 12 account, and that under the influence of the Lk. 10. 38-42 narrative, which he knew, he identified each with one of the sisters of the Luke narrative, and introduced the sister missing in each of the pericopes into the text. He is right, as we have seen, as regards 12. 1 ff.; but his position in connection with ch. 11 is untenable. Mary is not only mentioned in vv. 28-42 but in v. 45. And vv. 28-32, as Bultmann (*Das Evangelium des Johannes, ad loc.*) points out, cannot be detached from the account in its present form, since, by supplying a crowd of Jewish witnesses to the miracle, they provide the indispensable introduction to vv. 35-45, which, as over against vv. 17-27, retail the external miracle performed by Jesus to awaken belief in those who stand in need of such a demonstration of his power.

[2] That it was important to him to make this point is clear from the fact that he makes it not only here but in 11. 2. Though that verse is full of difficulties—for a list of them see the commentaries of Wellhausen, Bernard and Bultmann—to dismiss it as a late gloss, as those three commentators do, gives no more satisfactory a solution than such tactics usually do; it is

therefore justified in distinguishing in the Church's tradition a cycle of at least three stories existing prior to the activity of the evangelists, a cycle of—we may assume—originally oral tradition which was drawn on by two of them. We may further assert that this cycle was associated with the town of Bethany; this is clear from the fact that Mark locates his account of the anointing, which is a variant of one of the three Mary-Martha stories, in Bethany—and that John mentions that Lazarus came from Bethany, thus identifying not only his account of the anointing but also the raising of Lazarus with that village. [1]

---

better, lacking manuscript evidence to the contrary, to accept it as stemming from the evangelist. The chief difficulty of the verse, that it refers with an aorist-participial noun to an event which in John's gospel does not precede but follows, may be due to a characteristic inexactitude of the evangelist (cf. 1. 15, where the Baptist says that the Word is he about whom he John prophesied "he coming after me is before me, for he was before me," when in fact no such prophecy is previously recorded—further 14. 31 cf. 15. 1, 16. 12 cf. 15. 15), but is probably to be explained, with Blass-Debrunner (*Grammatik des neutestamentlichen Griechisch*, § 339. 1) on the basis of ἀλείψασα as here referring to a future action from the standpoint of the past, rendering the meaning of 11. 2 "Mary was she who, as is well known, later anointed the Lord." At any event the verse shows that John, though in his version of the anointing he collated three accounts, insisted upon the identity of the actors as derived from his non-synoptic source. He is not merely referring to Luke, assuming his readers' knowledge of Mary from that gospel; rather, since in Luke not Mary but a woman who was a sinner (whom Luke did not identify with Mary) anointed Jesus, he is correcting Luke in a manner analogous to his correction of Luke (and Mark) in 3. 24.

[1] Zurhellen, *op. cit.*, p. 43, suggests a further contact between Luke and John in connection with the Mary-Martha cycle in that he believes the name Lazarus in Luke's 16. 19-31 parable is secondary, being derived from the Johannine tradition of the raising of Lazarus. He points out the problematical nature of the name Lazarus, the only name of an individual appearing in Jesus' parables, and asserts that it, along with vv. 27-31, was later added to 16. 19-26, the point being to suggest in the reader's mind when he heard 16. 30 ("If someone—i.e. Lazarus—is raised from the dead and goes to them —i.e. the rich men's brothers—they will repent") that even when Lazarus *was* raised from the dead, the Jews didn't repent (cf. Lk. 16-31). But the separation of vv. 27-31 from vv. 19-26 cannot be carried through. Though the former doubtless represents a development of theme as over against vv. 19-26, where the point is that the lot of rich and poor in afterlife will be reversed, nevertheless the two parts are organically connected by the theme of the imperative importance of present charitable and unselfish behaviour. It is clear, then, that if (which is possible) Lazarus came to the parable from a Johannine tradition, it happened at an early stage of the parable's transmission, before Luke encountered it; this is confirmed by the fact that Luke, whose gospel contains no account of the raising of Lazarus, presumably did not know the story, so that he can certainly not have added the name to the parable.

We conclude, then, that John in his account of the anointing of Jesus derived the anointing, the drying of the hair and the note that Martha served from Luke's gospel, but that prior to both evangelists a cycle of three Mary-Martha stories existed on which both evangelists independently drew.

CHAPTER TWO

SPECULATION ABOUT JOHN THE BAPTIST

Luke 3.15 f. / John 1. 19, 27

The earliest similarity between passages in the two gospels occurs in connection with the material they offer on John the Baptist. Luke recounts (3. 15 f.) that the crowd wondered if John were the Christ, and John by way of answer spoke of the mightier one coming after him, the thongs of whose sandals he was not worthy to untie. The fourth gospel narrates (1. 19 f.) that the Jews sent priests and Levites to John to ask him who he was, whereupon he answered that he wasn't the Christ, and seven verses later referred to one coming after him whose sandals he was not worthy to untie. Moreover, in Acts (13. 25) Paul, in the course of a speech in the synagogue in Pisidian Antioch, refers to John's having said "I am not he whom you take me to be; but lo after me comes one whose sandals I am not worthy to untie". There are no verbal similarities between Luke and John here except as regards the statement about the shoes of the coming one; that, however, is found in the identical form in Mark and very likely also in Q (cf. Lk. 3. 7-9, 16b-17 and Mt. 3. 7-12), so does not constitute a special Lucan-Johannine element. What does constitute such an element is the connection of this statement with mention of speculation by the Jews as to who John was. In Luke's case the notice about such speculation, and therefore the connection between it and John's subsequent declaration, originated with the evangelist. [1] Luke in 3. 7-9, 16 f. utilized a block of Q material, into which he inserted 3. 10-14 (drawn by him from oral tradition); the resulting unevenness between the insertion and John's statement about the coming one he removed by means of an introduction to the latter which he composed (v. 15); [2] moreover, he employed

[1] So Loisy, *L'Evangile selon Luc*, *ad loc.*, Klostermann, *Das Lukasevangelium, ad loc.*, K. L. Schmidt, *Der Rahmen der Geschichte Jesu*, p. 27, Dibelius, *Die Urchristliche Ueberlieferung von Johannes dem Täufer*, p. 84, Bultmann, *Die Geschichte der synoptischen Tradition*, p. 359, Conzelmann, *Die Mitte der Zeit*, p. 12.

[2] Rengstorf, *Das Evangelium des Lukas, ad loc.*, attributes 3. 15 to a running Palestinian source which, following Schlatter, *op. cit.*, pp. 463-476,

the same combination of speculation and disclaimer elsewhere, in Acts 13. 25.

As for the fourth evangelist, though he knew Luke's gospel, the differences between him and Luke at this point are too great to postulate his dependence on Luke; further, the theme of the Baptist's witness to Jesus, of which his rejection of messianic pretentions forms a part, plays too important a rôle in John[1] for one to be justified in seeing John as deriving the latter from a source; rather v. 19 was composed by him to provide a setting in which the Baptist, in the following verses, could define his position.[2] It is possible that he mentioned Levites as among the questioners sent by the Jews because of their authority as regards matters of purification, which were here involved because of the question about baptism (v. 25);[3] at any event "priests and Levites" was a stock phrase coming readily to mind.[4] That is not to say that there was no speculation on the part of the Jews as to who John was, and specifically whether he was the messiah. Quite the contrary—historical fact lies at the root of the tradition which Luke and John, acting independently of one another, here bring. But this tradition had not already been written down. The evangelists, finding it as part of the oral tradition, and unconnected with the Baptist's statement about the mightier one following him, in joining it to the latter wrote it down for the first time.[5] As to where the two

---

he postulates that Luke used in addition to Mark and Matthew. We refer to the unsatisfactoriness of this theory below, p. 20, nt. 2; suffice it to say that such a theory does not do justice to the rôle oral tradition (from which, not from a running source, Luke derived 3. 10-14) plays, nor to Luke's rôle as an evangelist molding a gospel out of Mark, Q and oral tradition, which rôle necessitated his composing an introduction to the 3. 16 statement.

[1] Indeed Oscar Cullmann, in "L'opposition contre le Temple de Jerusalem motif commune de la theologie johannique et du monde ambiant," a paper read in September 1958 at the meeting of the Society of New Testament Studies in Strasbourg, maintains, partly on the basis of the evangelist's interest in the Baptist and in limiting his position to one of witness to Christ, that the fourth evangelist was an ex-disciple of the Baptist.

[2] So Kraeling, *John the Baptist*, p. 180, Barrett, *op. cit.*, *ad loc.*, Dibelius, *op. cit.*, p. 102, Bultmann, *Das Evangelium des Johannes*, *ad loc.*

[3] So Bultmann, *op. cit.*, *ad loc.*

[4] Cf. its use in the latter portions of the Old Testament, e.g. 1 Kings 8. 4, Ezra 1. 5, 2. 70, 3. 8, 1 Chron 28. 21, 2 Chron. 5. 5, 8. 15, 11. 13, 13. 9 f., 23. 4.

[5] It is not possible here to compare the whole body of material which Luke brings on the Baptist with that John brings, for that belongs in the domain of a comparison of their theologies, which is beyond the scope of the

evangelists encountered this oral tradition, we shall reserve discussion of this question, not only as regards this tradition but as regards all the Lucan-Johannine traditions we shall examine, till chapter thirteen.

The notes in Luke and John about the speculation as to the identity of the Baptist were, then, derived by the two evangelists independently of one another from oral tradition.

---

present work. Suffice it to say that, though John opposes himself sharply to Luke (and to Mark and Matthew) at one point (i.e. the dating of the Baptist's imprisonment: Jn. 3. 24 cf. Lk. 3. 19 f.), the same tendency to reduce the Baptist's position as over against that he holds in Mark and Matthew can be discerned in both Luke and John (a tendency not incompatible in John with his inclusion of non-synoptic Baptist traditions), a tendency reflected elsewhere in the New Testament in the fact that the Baptist is nowhere mentioned in it outside the gospels and Acts.

CHAPTER THREE

A MIRACULOUS CATCH OF FISH

Luke 5. 1-11 / John 21. 1-14

Both the third and the fourth gospels contain accounts of miraculous catches of fish, with these elements in common: the scene (the Sea of Galilee), Peter and the sons of Zebedee as participants, the catch following a night of unsuccessful fishing, the catch at Jesus' command. Yet equally striking are the divergences. In Luke Jesus is in the boat which catches the fish, two boats in all are involved, and the incident culminates in Jesus' call of Peter to discipleship; in John the need for food is stressed, only one boat is mentioned, Jesus remains on shore, the fishing is concluded by a meal, above all, the whole scene constitutes a resurrection appearance. A direct relation between the two accounts, i.e. literary dependence of one on the other, is excluded by the fact that only two significant words are common to both: ἰχθύς and δίκτυον. That is to say, though the fourth evangelist knew the Lucan passage he has not grafted elements from it into the related passage in his own gospel. A connection between the two can only be a matter of a connection at an earlier stage in the transmission of the tradition, before the two stories were parts of the two gospels. And the question to be asked is whether in either of the two accounts the connection of the miracle with its context is tenuous; if so this would show that its original context was in the other account. For this purpose we shall examine both passages, beginning with the Johannine.

It is characterized by a striking internal difficulty, i.e. the fact that the disciples, having caught at Jesus' command an enormous catch of fish (ἰχθύες), on coming ashore find other fish (ὀψάριον) and bread awaiting them; and they eat the latter, not what they've caught. On the basis of this, Schwartz [1] sees the fishing element as secondary, having originally nothing to do with the resurrection story which (preserved according to him in vv. 1-3, 4a, 9, 12-13) narrated (a) the appearance of the Lord to the disciples who've

[1] In the *Zeitschrift für die Neutestamentliche Wissenschaft*, 1914, pp. 216 f.

fled to Galilee and resumed their occupation, and (b) his renewal of the table fellowship with them. But Bultmann[1] refutes this with the observation that the detailed description in v. 3, and above all the ἐπίασεν οὐδέν, are both inseparable from v. 5, to which they lead up. Goguel[2] affirms that the miraculous catch of Jn. 21 originally was followed merely by a meal and had nothing to do with a resurrection appearance until it was later joined to a story, similar to the Emmaus one, in which the resurrected Jesus made himself known to his disciples in breaking bread with them. But this explanation fails to take account of the fact that the recognition of Jesus in Jn. 21 stems exclusively from the fishing incident and has nothing to do with eating. The fact that in Luke's gospel a resurrection account centering about recognition through table fellowship exists (Lk. 24. 13-35) does not justify us, in the absence of compelling evidence in the Jn. 21 text, in seeing a similar story as the core of these verses.

It is clear, then, that at the core of 21. 1-14 lies the miraculous catch and the recognition of the resurrected Jesus rising out of it. There is good reason to believe that this was originally the first appearance of the risen Christ and not the third (or fourth), as it is in its present Johannine form. For this speak the following: (a) the disciples in Jn. 21. 1 ff. have returned to their fishing, which precludes a previous resurrection appearance of Jesus to them; (b) the disciples do not recognize Jesus as they would if he had already appeared to them since his resurrection; (c) 20. 29 implies that the present position of the Jn. 21 resurrection appearance is not the original one: the third appearance in ch. 20 was originally the last one recounted in the gospel—and this is confirmed by 20. 30 f., which clearly formed the conclusion to the gospel in its original (perhaps unpublished) form; (d) 21. 14 lends itself well to the view that the evangelist, when incorporating 21. 1-13 into the gospel, [3] here (and in the addition of πάλιν in 21. 1 and of elements of 21. 7) altered a written account of the event in which it constituted the first resurrection appearance. [4]

---

[1] Bultmann, *op. cit.*, *ad loc.*

[2] Goguel, *The Birth of Christianity*, pp. 51 f.

[3] That ch. 21 stems from the same hand as ch. 1-20 (though, as 20. 30 f. shows, added later as a supplement) has been demonstrated by Bernard, *op. cit.*, *ad loc.*, with his statistics on the extraordinary closeness in style of 21. 1-14 to ch. 20.

[4] Though we can determine this, the passage remains problematic. The

Two elements in Luke's passage speak for the fact that the fishing miracle of Luke is dependent upon the tradition of a first appearance lying behind Jn. 21. First, Peter's statement 'depart from me, for I am a sinner, Lord" in v. 8 makes more sense than it presently does if it was originally part of a resurrection appearance and, as such, came after Peter's denial of Jesus. Second, Σίμων Πέτρος in v. 8 indicates dependence on a Johannine tradition, for this, the usual Johannine form (found in Jn. 21. 2, 7, 11) is never otherwise found in Luke, [1] who, indeed, first explains the name Πέτρος in 6. 14.

We must now ask if the fishing miracle in Luke can be shown to be detachable from its context; if it can, we may be sure that its position in Luke as over against that in John is secondary. The Lucan passage consists of three parts, the teaching from a boat, the fishing miracle, and the call of Peter. The miracle can, as a matter of fact, be detached without difficulty from the first part: the crowd disappears in v. 4 as suddenly as the teaching motif does. [2] The matter of the connection of the fishing and the call is not so simple, due to the presence of a Marcan parallel (in 1. 16 f.) in the story of Jesus' call of Peter, Andrew and the sons of Zebedee. The question therefore arises whether Lk. 5. 4-11 can be divided into two parts, one, vv. 4-9, going back to a Johannine and the other, vv. 10 f., to a Marcan tradition. A comparison of the forms of the call in Luke (μὴ φοβοῦ· ἀπὸ τοῦ νῦν ἀνθρώπους ἔσῃ ζωγρῶν) and in Mk. 1. 16 f. (δεῦτε ὀπίσω μου, καὶ ποιήσω ὑμᾶς γενέσθαι ἁλεεῖς ζωγρῶν)

---

extent to which John altered his source, thereby introducing into it some of the present unevenness (for one instance of this see nt. 11 below), is not fully clear. Presumably the sudden energence of the beloved disciple in v. 7 is due to him; there is, however, no compelling reason to attribute to his editing the confusing fact that Peter's arrival at the shore is not mentioned, though that of the others, whom presumably in his impulsive fashion he precedes, is. In v. 5, as in Lk. 24. 41, Jesus asks if the disciples have anything to eat; it is conceivable that John in editing the story has drawn on this Lucan element, though the fact that the vocabulary of the Johannine statement is different from that of the Lucan means that, if he did so, he did so from memory.

[1] Nor is it read here by all the manuscripts, though as the *lectio difficilior* it is certainly original.

[2] 5. 1-3 is strikingly similar to Mk. 4. 1 f., which latter Luke does not adduce at the corresponding place in this gospel. It is conceivable that 5. 1-3 already constituted the introduction to the fishing miracle when Luke encountered it, and he therefore suppressed Mk. 4. 1 f.; but it is far more likely that, on the basis of Mk. 4. 1 f., he composed an introduction to the miracle.

shows that there is no direct relation between the two; what is common to them is that (a) in both Jesus' call to discipleship is a pun on the profession of the men he is calling; (b) in both accounts Peter and the sons of Zebedee are called; (c) in Luke the disciples leave (ἀφίημι) all and follow Jesus, and in Mark the sons of Zebedee leave (ἀφίημι) their nets. The first of these similarities is surely only to be explained on the basis of a common root, at a point more or less removed from the accounts in their present form.

However, in order to trace Lk. 5. 4-11 back to a Marcan and a Johannine tradition, it must be shown that it can be divided into two parts. But this is impossible to do. What binds the two so strongly together is the important rôle Peter has; Dibelius [1] goes so far as to say that the decisive interest here is not in the call of the disciples but in Peter as the most important of disciples and Christians. The absolutely preeminent rôle of Peter among the fishermen (see vv. 3, 4, 5, 8, 10) is graphically illustrated in the notable fact that though all the fishermen leave everything and follow Jesus, Peter alone (v. 10 ἔσῃ) is called. [2] This rôle for Peter is wholly lacking in the Marcan call, where he is merely one of the four fishermen called, all of whom are mentioned by name. That the Peter motif was created by the third evangelist who used it to bind the fishing and the call together is excluded by the obviously extrinsic position of the sons of Zebedee in v. 10. This position is explicable only on the basis of the evangelist's addition of the sons of Zebedee to a story which he took over (in which only Peter was named) in order to make it more suitable for his purposes, i.e. as a replacement for the Marcan call, [3] where the sons of Zebedee are on a par with Peter. [4]

If two elements, one of which we later encounter in Mark and one in John, were combined, it was done at an early stage, probably before they had been written down, and we can no longer trace the process. We cannot even be absolutely sure it took place at all; Peter's reaction, for instance, though strikingly well accounted for on the basis of its following on his denial of Christ, is plausibly

[1] Dibelius, *From Tradition to Gospel*, p. 113.

[2] This imbalance is clearly the explanation for the D variant reading of vv. 10 f.

[3] So Dibelius, *op. cit.*, p. 112, and Loisy, *op. cit.*, *ad loc.*

[4] The fact that the sons of Zebedee and the fishermen follow Jesus, though only Peter is called, is to be similarly explained, since in the Marcan pericope all four fishermen are called by and follow Jesus.

explained in Luke's account on the basis of his numinous dread of the miracle-worker in whom he senses the divine power of judgment; [1] and the close inner relation of the events of the fishing miracle to the call—the former preceding, and authenticating, the latter [2]—compel us to reckon with the possibility that the miracle *was* originally connected with the call of the disciples. [3] But it is exceedingly unlikely that Jesus performed two such similar miracles at different times. One of the two accounts must be secondary. And the fact that we have in Mark a parallel, related version of the call where the miracle plays no part militates powerfully against the Lucan version. We conclude, then, though the evidence is not undivided, [4] that Luke's context for the miracle is secondary as

[1] Loisy's argument (*op. cit., ad loc.*) that κύριε in v. 8 presupposes that Peter had already been a disciple is not valid, for Peter's use of the word is fully appropriate on the occasion of his becoming a disciple—quite apart from the fact that in 5. 12 and 19. 41 κύριε is used as a term of address to Jesus by non-disciples. Klostermann's citation (*op. cit. ad loc.*) of Judg. 6. 22 and Isa. 6. 5 as parallels is therefore a legitimate one.

[2] Peter, that is to say, is not only called, but ordained. It is such a consideration that leads Bultmann, *op. cit., ad loc.*, to see the Jn. 21 resurrection appearance as originally concluding with a commissioning by Jesus of the disciples to apostleship.

[3] It has been maintained that a third consideration against Luke's version here being secondary to John's is to be found in the fact that the nets in Luke, which break, clearly do not signify the Church, whereas in John, where it is explicitly stated that the net (singular, no longer plural) did not break, the net does signify the Church—and that the greater degree of allegorization of the John account militates against its primariness. But this is to confuse the present form of the text with its history. In all likelihood the fourth evangelist here corrected the Lucan account, because he understood the net to mean the Church. (That he also inserted the number of the fish caught, 153, is clear because, though it has never been satisfactorily explained, the number must have allegorical significance; further, the fact that Peter brings the fish to Jesus, though Jesus commands the other fishermen to do so and though Peter's arrival on shore is not mentioned, stems from the evangelist's understanding Peter's action as that of the head of the Church.) But this does not mean that the Johannine account, except in its final form, is newer than the Lucan account—which is in any event the case in view of the fact that John wrote later than Luke. We see here an example of the fact that John was freer in rewriting his sources than Luke was. For Luke in all likelihood also saw the miracle as having an allegorical significance, as prefiguring the successful institution of the mission to the Gentiles (for Luke Peter was the first leader of the Gentile mission: see Acts 10 f.)—hence as related to the preceding 4. 16-30, which symbolize the rejection of the Church by the Jews (so correctly Creed, *The Gospel according to St. Luke, ad loc.*). But, less thorough here than John, he did not carry through the allegorization into the details, and so left the detail of the breaking net unaltered.

[4] A graphic proof of the dividedness of the evidence is that, whereas in

over against John's. Furthermore, the occurrence of the form Σίμων Πέτρος in the Lucan account points to it either as arising out of, or at some point in its trasmission associated with, a milieu where Peter was known as Σίμων Πέτρος, a milieu which we label Johannine because this form is otherwise known to us only through its use by the fourth evangelist. [1]

---

his commentary on John (p. 546) Bultmann maintains that the John context, i. e. a resurrection appearance, is the original one, in the *Geschichte der synoptischen Tradition* p. 232 he sees the Johannine version as later than, and "somehow" going back to, Luke.

[1] Before we approach the accounts of the passion we must mention one more parallel, though due to its lack of importance we may do so in a footnote. The parallel, between Lk. 7. 1-10 and Jn. 4. 46-53, to which Schniewind, *op. cit.*, pp. 16 ff., unjustifiably attributes much importance, is robbed of real significance by the fact that Matthew also contains an account of a healing (associated with Capernaum) by Jesus of the absent dependent of an official, and that Luke's and John's accounts have nothing of any importance in common with each other which is not shared by Matthew. Luke's source here was the same (written) one—part of the Q cycle of tradition—as Matthew's, as a comparison of Lk. 7. 6-9 and Mt. 8. 8-10 shows. As for John, as we know, he knew Luke's gospel, and so Luke's account; from his memory of it (the parallels in no way justify us in assuming he consulted it when composing his passage) he may have been—unconsciously—influenced to use the words ἀκούειν, ἐρωτᾶν and μέλλειν (coupled with ἀποθνήσκειν in his gospel, in Luke with τελευτᾶν)—though it is more likely that these agreements are all accidental. He draws, at any event, to a far greater extent on a tradition known to him according to which the official in question was a βασιλικός, his son (not his servant) was ill, he sought Jesus out in Cana, and the boy was healed in the very hour in which Jesus assured the father that he would be healed. (It is true that Matthew's account also offers this last, but it is unlikely that John knew Matthew, and such a feature is to be expected in a story of a healing at a distance, and so was probably part of John's special source.) One fact remains to be noted. John's account (5. 43) contains the statement that, upon the official's learning of his son's healing, he and his whole house believed. This striking expression is found elsewhere in the New Testament only in Acts (16. 31-33, 18. 8 and in slightly different form in 10. 2, 11. 4); either it stems here from the evangelist (he does not, to be sure, use it elsewhere, but that may be merely because he nowhere else discusses a man who comes to believe in Jesus a member of whose family is mentioned) or from his source; it indicates that to either John or his source the missionary terminology of the Acts milieu was familiar.

CHAPTER FOUR

LUKE'S AND JOHN'S PASSION ACCOUNTS

A Word of Introduction

There are, in comparison with the earlier parts of the gospels, a large number of contacts between the Lucan and Johannine accounts of the passion and resurrection. By way of background, a few remarks on the passion accounts of both gospels are in order.

The literary composition of both Luke's and John's passion and resurrection narratives is not so easy to determine as that of Matthew, who followed Mark very closely at this point, merely adding a few easily identifiable passages, [1] until he came to Mk. 16. 8, whereupon he added his own tradition of the resurrection appearances. By contrast, Luke's procedure is here problematical. His account of the passion contains a great deal of non-Marcan material, e.g. the account of the institution of the eucharist, [2] the Lucan "last discourse" in 22. 21-38, the account of Pilate's behaviour at Jesus' trial, the hearing before Herod, Jesus' remarks to the women of Jerusalem on his way to Golgotha, the incident of the varying reactions to Jesus of the two criminals crucified with him (23. 39-42), Jesus' word to one of them (v. 43), his dying word (v. 46). [3] Furthermore, Luke's account contains no fewer than fourteen changes of order as over against Mark's. [4]

These facts have given rise to theories, the most recent that of Streeter [5] and Taylor [6], according to which Luke's primary source

[1] i. e. the death of Judas, Pilate's wife's dream, Pilate's handwashing.

[2] See the arguments, convincing in the opinion of the writer, in Jeremias' *The Eucharistic Words of Jesus*, pp. 102 f., for Luke's use at this point of a liturgical text which included vv. 19 b-20.

[3] As for Jesus' first word from the cross (23. 34), the textual evidence is too inconclusive for us to be able to determine with certainty whether or not it belongs to Luke's original gospel. See further on this below, p. 81, nt. 1.

[4] Taylor, *Behind the Third Gospel*, p. 73, offers a partial list of these.

[5] Streeter, *op. cit.*, pp. 201-222.

[6] Taylor, *op. cit.*, 1926. A third proponent of such theories who should be mentioned is A. M. Perry, author of *The Sources of Luke's Passion-Narrative*, 1920. Taylor acknowledges his indebtedness to Perry, but in connection with a summarization of Perry's views (*op. cit.*, pp. 20 ff.) outlines his criticisms of them, criticisms in which the present writer concours.

for the passion was not Mark but another document into which Marcan elements (above all, numerous phrases) have been inserted. [1] The Streeter-Taylor hypothesis sees Luke's special passion-resurrection source as a part of a source (which the two call proto-Luke) running through the whole gospel, a source written by the evangelist (before he knew Mark) from traditions special to him and from Q, to which he later added large sections of Mark. This hypothesis in its totality concerns us, for virtually all the Lucan contacts with John come in the sections which Streeter and Taylor, and following them Easton, [2] attribute to proto-Luke. These include the miraculous catch, the healing of the centurion's servant, [3] and the anointing of Jesus by the woman who was a sinner.

Despite the good points of the hypothesis, [4] it does not stand the test of criticism. The blocks which are supposed to constitute the source don't fit together well; [5] even more significant, 9. 50-18. 14, with its character of an aimless journey, is not suited to be the central section of a gospel, whereas 8. 4-9. 50 (which includes Peter's confession, the transfiguration and the first two predictions of the passion), taken over from Mark, is. This suggests that Mark and not the non-Marcan sections of Luke forms the core of Luke's gospel. [6] It is therefore preferable to regard Mark as forming the

[1] In this way an attempt is made to account for the fact that despite wide variance of the Lucan from the Marcan passion accounts there is verbal evidence of Mark in Luke's text in every single pericope except the account of the crucifixion.

[2] Easton, *The Gospel according to St. Luke*, 1926.

[3] According to Easton, *ibid, ad loc.*, only vv. 2-6a and 10 derive from proto-Luke.

[4] Except for 5. 1-11, the non-Marcan elements of Luke come in blocks (which supports the view that originally they belonged together in a continuous source): 1. 1-4. 30, 6. 20-8. 3, 9. 51-18. 14, 19. 1-28, in none of which are there traces of Mark, though this isn't true for the last block, 22. 14—end. Further, the view that not Mark but proto-Luke forms the basis of the gospel explains the omission of Mk. 6. 42-8. 26 *en bloc* from Luke as well as the frequent cases (for a list of such, see H. K. Luce's *The Gospel according to S. Luke*, p. xxvi) in which Luke prefers Q or his own special material to Marcan material).

[5] For example, the connection between 5. 1-11 and 6. 12 (Taylor, *op. cit.*, pp. 168 f., claims 6. 12-19 for proto-Luke) is very difficult; in 6. 12 ff. the choosing of the twelve from the disciples is recorded, but, in what Taylor reckons as proto-Luke, there has been no previous mention of disciples except for Peter and the sons of Zebedee.

[6] This is confirmed by an analysis of the Lucan journey section; for example (as Conzelmann, *op. cit.*, p. 59 nt. 3, points out) the fact that the non-Marcan Zacchaeus story follows the Marcan account of the healing of

core of Luke, to which non-Marcan material from various sources [1] was added in blocks by the evangelist. [2] This is not only true for the gospel as a whole, it is true also for its passion account. Luke, as we shall see, does present considerable special material here—e.g. an account of the approach to Jerusalem, of the institution of the eucharist, of the events of the last supper, of Jesus' examination by the Jews. But some of it came to him in oral, some in written form; we have no evidence that it—or elements of it—ever constituted a continuous passion source, whereas we find traces of Mark's account in every single section of the passion, which justifies the view that Luke had only one running source for the passion, Mark's gospel. [3] His departures from Mark are by no means all to be explained as due to his introduction of other written or oral elements known to him; his own editorial recasting of material, as we shall see, plays an important rôle. [4]

As for John, in his account of the passion he is closer to the synoptic gospels than elsewhere. [5] The reason for this lies in the nature of the material in question, [6] which curtailed John's independence at this point. It is certain that John drew on Mark here as a source; [7] he also used Luke—to a far greater degree, as we shall

---

Bartimaeus, being tacked on to it through 19. 1, shows that the Marcan material not the non-Marcan forms the core here; if the latter were the case, the Bartimaeus story would follow the Zacchaeus account.

[1] One of them was the special Jerusalem source of the infancy narratives, another was Q — the latter in written form, as a comparison of Lk. 7. 66-9 and Mt. 8. 8-10 shows.

[2] Therewith fall not only Streeter's and Taylor's theories, but the related one of Schlatter, *op. cit.*, pp. 463 ff., who maintains that, though Luke knew Mark and Matthew, the backbone of his gospel was a Palestinian source from which, for example, he drew the entire travel section and—what not even Taylor maintains—the infancy narratives.

[3] So correctly Gilmour, *The Gospel according to St. Luke*, p. 17, Creed, *op. cit.*, p. lviii, nt. 1, and Bultmann, *Geschichte der synoptischen Tradition*, p. 298.

[4] It accounts for at least eight of the fourteen changes in order—on five of which see below, pp. 113 f.

[5] In common with them he has an account of Jesus' last meal, of the arrest outside Jerusalem (manifestly in the same place, though described differently), of a hearing before the high priest and Pilate, of Peter's denial, the crucifixion and the finding of the empty tomb.

[6] The account of the passion in all probability crystallized earlier into an oral and then a literary whole than the other gospel material, and so took more unified, and authoritative, form: so Bultmann, *op. cit.*, pp. 297 ff., and Dibelius, *From Tradition to Gospel*, pp. 178 ff.

[7] We saw this in connection with the story of the anointing in Bethany. In addition, the reaching of vinegar to Jesus immediately before his death, Jn. 19. 29 f. cf. Mk. 15. 36, may be cited.

see, than Mark. Nevertheless, at a number of points [1] he departs from the synoptic tradition. Though a portion of these departures, as we shall see, stem from John himself, nevertheless he also unquestionably draws on nonsynoptic sources—e.g. in the approach to Jerusalem, in the last supper scene, and in the hearing before the high priest. This leads Dibelius [2] and Bultmann [3] to assert that John's primary source for the passion (and resurrection) was a running account otherwise unknown to us, rather than any of the other gospels. But, quite apart from the fact that this fails to take account of his use of Mark and Luke, it assumes that the isolated pieces of non-synoptic tradition to which the evidence of John's account points may be seen as parts of a continuing source—for which assumption there is no evidence at all, as Bultmann himself admits. [4] Lacking such evidence, it is wiser to refrain from such an assumption. [5]

We maintain, then, that neither Luke nor John had a continuous non-synoptic source for their passion accounts. Aware that only in the course of exegesis conducted in terms of this position can its merits be revealed, we turn to an examination of the portions of the Lucan and Johannine accounts of the passion which are or appear to be parallel.

---

[1] e.g. the footwashing at the last supper, the hearings before both Annas and Caiaphas, the scourging of Jesus by Pilate in the midst of the trial, the location of the trial in Gabbatha, the bone-breaking incident, and the words from the cross. For a full list, see Gardner-Smith, *op. cit.*, pp. 57 f.

[2] Dibelius, "Die alttestamentliche Motive in der Leidengeschichte des Petrus- und des Johannesevangeliums," *Zeitschrift für die Alttestamentliche Wissenschaft*, Supplement 33, pp. 125-150.

[3] Bultmann, *Das Evangelium des Johannes*, p. 491.

[4] *ibid.* Dibelius' arguments (*op. cit.*) in this regard are not convincing.

[5] The result of Bultmann's error is that he attributes to this hypothetical source a great deal which, as we shall see, John actually derives from Luke's gospel.

CHAPTER FIVE

THE APPROACH TO JERUSALEM

Luke 19. 37-40 / John 12. 12-19

The Lucan and Johannine accounts of Jesus' approach to Jerusalem [1] contain the following common elements, none of which appear in Mark or Matthew: (a) in both cases the acclamation is connected with Jesus' activity as a miracle-worker: in Luke (19. 37) the disciples acclaim Jesus because of the wonders which they have seen him perform, in John (12. 17 f.) the crowd acclaims him because of the raising of Lazarus; (b) in the words of acclamation of both gospels, βασιλέυς is part of the sentence following on the first εὐλογημένος, and βασιλεύς is in apposition to ὁ ἐρχόμενος; [2] (c) in both cases (Lk. 19. 39 f. and Jn. 12. 19) the Pharisees are mentioned as reacting negatively to the acclamation. [3]

[1] For our purpose it is convenient to include Jesus' approach with those passages belonging more immediately to the account of the passion, a procedure justified in John's case, where the entry (Jn 12. 12-19) follows mention of the priests' plot (11. 53), whereas in Luke the order of these two events is reversed, and the cleansing of the temple and the account of Jesus' teaching in Jerusalem intervene between them.

[2] F. C. Grant, *op. cit.*, p. 294, tentatively supported by Streeter, *op. cit.*, p. 404, sees βασιλέυς as an insertion in Luke's text, and cites W's reading, in which βασιλεύς doesn't appear, in support of his view. But this is incorrect. B's awkward appositional reading is certainly the *lectio difficilior*; all the other readings (including W, which returns to the simpler Marcan version) represent efforts to produce a smoother text. B is accepted as the best reading by Nestle, *Novum Testamentum Graece*, and by Creed, Easton and Klostermann in their commentaries. —In Jn. 12. 13, the *koine* omits καὶ ὁ, so that βασιλεύς is no longer in apposition to but is modified by ὁ ἐρχόμενος κτλ., but this clearly constitutes a secondary effort to produce a less awkward text.

[3] Wellhausen, *Das Evangelium Lucae*, *ad loc.*, sees the words τῶν Φαρισαίων as a secondary interpolation, citing in support their omission in the Sinai Syriac translation. But no other manuscripts omit these words, and, as we shall see below, the presence of the Pharisees presents difficulties which would explain their omission in the Sinai Syriac. Creed, *op. cit.*, *ad loc.*, cites Matthew as containing a corresponding scene as far as the Pharisees' reaction is concerned in 21. 15 f.; but, though the similarities between the Lucan and Matthean text are striking, there is one important difference: in Luke the occasion of this hostility is the acclimation of Jesus on his approach to Jerusalem on the basis of miracles he has earlier performed, whereas in Matthew the occasion is the acclamation of Jesus by children (παῖδες) in

Have we evidence either of direct dependence of John's account on Luke's, or of a common source for the two? Before we can answer this, we must be aware of the differences which exist between the two accounts. In Luke (as in Mark) the account of the entry is preceded by the finding of the young animal (πῶλος) which Jesus then mounts, Jesus is acclaimed by the disciples accompanying him, and the Pharisees, objecting, ask Jesus to rebuke his followers. In John, on the other hand, pilgrims in Jerusalem for the feast come out to acclaim the approaching Jesus, whereupon it is briefly stated that Jesus finds and mounts a young ass (ὀνάριον) according to the prophecy of Zech. 9. 9, and the Pharisees, objecting to the acclamation, do not speak to Jesus but rather among themselves. Moreover, as regards the rôle Jesus' previous wonders play, there is no verbal similarity—Luke has the word δυνάμεις, John has ὅτε τὸν Λάζαρον ἐφώνησεν κτλ.

The two passages, then, evince both marked similarities and dissimilarities. Let us begin our attempt to figure out their relation by taking a closer look at the agreement as regards βασιλεύς. In Luke the first sentence of the acclamation is εὐλογημένος ὁ ἐρχόμενος ὁ βασιλεὺς ἐν ὀνόματι κυρίου. In John it is ὡσαννά, εὐλογημένος ὁ ἐρχόμενος ἐν ὀνόματι κυρίου, καὶ ὁ βασιλεὺς τοῦ Ισραήλ. This similarity would be striking were it not for the closeness to both of Mark's text (11. 9): ὡσαννά, εὐλογημένος ὁ ἐρχόμενος ἐν ὀνόματι κυρίου· εὐλογημένη ἡ ἐρχομένη βασιλεία τοῦ πατρὸς ἡμῶν Δαυιδ κτλ.; and indeed the question of the connection between Luke's and John's accounts cannot be answered until we have examined the question of the relation of both passages to Mark.

The commentators are divided in their opinion as to what is Luke's primary source in 19. 37 f. [1] Those critics who believe it was Mark [2] hold that Luke as regards his use of βασιλεύς is not following an independent source, but rather compressing Mk. 11. 9b

---

Jerusalem in the temple because of healings he has performed there after first casting out the money changers.

Schniewind, *op. cit.*, p. 27, sees a further parallel between John and Luke in that in each the disciples play a special rôle. But in Luke their rôle is that of acclamation, whereas in John it is the crowd who fills that rôle; the disciples in John's account are mentioned only in 12. 16, and then in another connection.

[1] These are the verses which contain the reference to miracles and the words of acclimation; the reference to the Pharisees follows in vv. 39 f.

[2] So Creed and Klostermann, in their commentaries, Grant, *op. cit.*, p. 294, and Dibelius, *Theologische Literaturzeitung*, 1927, p. 148.

and 10a into one sentence, thereby producing the awkward apposition of 19. 38a. [1] There is no doubt that in Luke's text βασιλεύς has been inserted into a quotation from psalm 118. 26 (LXX 117. 26); the question is whether Luke did this, or whether it was done by his source. The awkwardness of Lk. 19. 38 speaks against the verse's being a product of Luke's literary activity, for the evangelist is not noted for stylistic clumsiness. [2] In addition, it is to be noted that this is not the only divergence from Mark in vv. 37-39. There is the mention of the Mount of Olives, the cry ἐν οὐρανῷ εἰρήνη καὶ δόξα ἐν ὑψίστοις. There is, further, the mention of the δυνάμεις which we've already noted. The motivation for the acclamation of the δυνάμεις is problematical. The only miracle which has been recorded since the healing of the ten lepers on the borders of Samaria and Galilee (17. 11), i.e. nowhere near Jerusalem, is the healing of the blind man outside Jericho (18. 35-43). Why, one may ask, do the miracles have this delayed effect? [3] The Lucan text (Mark in 11. 8 has πολλοί) mentions a multitude of disciples (τὸ πλῆθος τῶν μαθητῶν) who acclaim Jesus on his approach to Jerusalem. Have a large number of disciples been accompanying Jesus on his way to Jerusalem? The Lucan account of the journey does not indicate this. This, however, would appear to be implied, as Jesus, coming according to Luke for the first time to Jerusalem, can have had no disciples there, or anyway no large group of them. The Johannine parallel has none of these difficulties. Jesus had very recently raised Lazarus from the dead, and had often since the beginning of his ministry been active in and near Jerusalem; to read in John of a multitude of his disciples near Jerusalem would be no surprise. Furthermore, the mention in Luke in v. 40 of Pharisees in the crowd of Jesus' disciples is surprising; in John, however, mention of them among the crowd of pilgrims coming from Jerusalem to meet Jesus is, in view of Jn. 11. 46 ff., not

[1] The reason for Luke's procedure Klostermann, *op. cit.*, *ad loc.*, and Conzelmann, *op. cit.*, p. 62, see in Lk. 19. 11.

[2] Creed, *op. cit.*, *ad loc.*, sees in the absense of ὡσαννά in this verse an indication that Luke, not a source, was responsible for its present form—for he sees the omission as due to Luke's well-known dislike of Semitic words. The omission can also be explained, however, on the basis of the utilization here by the author of Luke's source of the Septuagint, where ὡσαννά doesn't appear.

[3] It is undoubtedly because of this difficulty that the Sinai Syriac translation deletes δυνάμεων, and that D and one of the Latin translations substitute γινομένων.

surprising. We have, in fact, in vv. 37 f. and the two following verses, a passage based on a non-Marcan source, [1] a passage which presupposes the situation as we find it in John's gospel, but not in Luke's—and βασιλεύς was already inserted into Ps. 118. 25 in the source.

In the case of Jn. 12. 12, the majority critical verdict is that John is here using Mark as his source. [2] This view holds that the non-Marcan elements were added by John in his recasting of his source. So Grant [3] holds that the title βασιλεύς was introduced by John from the Zech. 9. 9 quotation which he adds two verses later to the text. But this reasoning is difficult to follow; if βασιλεύς was added by John to his gospel in the Zech. 9. 9 quote, why did he add it elsewhere? And why add βασιλεὺς τοῦ 'Ισραήλ, and not merely βασιλεύς? A more convincing explanation is that John found βασιλεὺς τοῦ θεοῦ already in his (non-Marcan) source. Furthermore, there are other indications that John here was not following Mark. The acclaimers in John's account are not disciples accompanying Jesus towards Jerusalem, but pilgrims from Jerusalem coming to meet him. These latter are not what the reader expects; after the mention of the Jews in v. 9, come out from Jerusalem to Bethany to see Jesus and Lazarus, we expect to read that the same group accompanied Jesus back to Jerusalem and entered the city with him the next day. The very unexpectedness of the statement in v. 12 shows that it stems not from John but from a source. [4] A non-Marcan source is indicated, [5] to which belonged the sentence of acclamation and the notice about the Pharisees. The connection of the acclamation to the raising of Lazarus (12. 17 f.) is due,

[1] This view is shared by Taylor, *op. cit.*, pp. 94 f., Easton, *op. cit.*, *ad loc.*, and Luce, *op. cit.*, pp. 297 f. It is not without its difficulties. All are agreed that Luke in 19. 28-36 is following Mark; why, the question presents itself, would Luke suddenly, after v. 36 which, at least in Mark, constitutes the introduction to the acclamation account, change to another source for an account of the remainder of it? Because of this difficulty Dibelius, *op. cit.*, p. 148, and Creed, *op. cit.*, *ad loc.*, see Mark as the only source for Luke in vv. 28-36. But a glance at a gospel harmony shows the improbability of this for vv. 37 f. Above all, 37a has the appearance of a seam, indicating the beginning of a new source.

[2] So Barrett, Hoskyns and Klostermann in their commentaries, and Grant, *op. cit.*, p. 294.

[3] Grant, *ibid.*

[4] So Bultmann, *op. cit.*, *ad loc.*

[5] So correctly Bultmann, *op. cit.*, *ad loc.*, and Dibelius, *From Tradition to Gospel*, p. 204, nt. 1.

however, to John; mention of the latter does not occur in v. 12, where we would expect it to, and its mention in vv. 17 f. is due to the evangelist, who in v. 17 connects the crowd of v. 12 to the preceding Lazarus miracle, and in v. 18 incorporates the crowd mentioned in v. 9, but passed over in 12, into the account of the acclamation. [1]

We are now in a position to be able to determine whether John's source here was Luke's gospel; whether, failing that, Luke and John have here a common source; or whether we must seek still another explanation of the similarities between the two gospel accounts. As to the first of these possibilities, the answer is clearly negative: John derived the notice about the pilgrims coming out of Jerusalem to meet Jesus from his source; since Luke's gospel does not contain this notice, it cannot have been John's source. As regards the second possibility, there is, to be sure, a certain verbal agreement between the two as regards the position of βασιλεύς in the sentence of acclamation. In Luke, however, ὁ βασιλεύς precedes ἐν ὀνόματι κυρίου, whereas in John it follows that phrase, and is coupled with τοῦ Ἰσραήλ. Considering how close both are to Mark and Matthew at this point, we are not justified in postulating dependence of both here on the same written source. [2] And the differences between Luke and John listed above confirm the fact that Luke and John did not here have the same source.

The solution to the problem of the relationship here between Luke and John is rather that each had a different non-Marcan source, which, however, agreed on a number of points. Furthermore, we can determine that both Luke's and John's sources were known to them only as isolated passges, accounts of the entry into Jerusalem alone, and not as parts of continuous sources. Luke does not record the miracles to which his source refers; we may therefore be certain that the source as it came to him did not include an account of the performing of these miracles, or else Luke would have recorded them in his gospel. That is to say, the source as Luke

---

[1] So correctly Bultmann, *op. cit.*, *ad loc.* John does this even at the price of producing a conflict between the different crowds of v. 17 and v. 18, for DE*L it sy's reading of ὅτι for ὅτε in 17, whereby the two crowds are identified, is clearly secondary.

[2] The position of βασιλεύς in Luke and John has, then, more negative than positive significance; though it does not lead us to postulate a common written source for Luke and John, it helps demonstrate that neither Luke nor John were following Mark at this point.

knew it must have begun with v. 37. It may have continued after v. 40, including vv. 41-44, though it is more likely that Luke found this prediction of Jerusalem's destruction circulating by itself and fitted it into his account at this point. Indeed, it is conceivable that the source as Luke knew it continued still further, but it is most unlikely—for in that case why did not Luke continue to use it rather than go back to Mark, which he follows from v. 45 until ch. 21? Lacking any evidence of its continuation, it is wiser to conclude that Luke knew this source as a fragment, in use as a lectionary or for catechetical purposes.

As for John's source, it contained as we saw no reference to the raising of Lazarus, the last preceding event in the gospel for which the evangelist drew on a source; moreover, the unexpectedness after v. 9 of the group mentioned in v. 12 proves that v. 12 (except for τῇ ἐπαύριον, which the evangelist added when incorporating the passage into his gospel) formed the beginning of the source as John knew it. Moreover, that it did not continue beyond this one scene is made likely by the fragmentary nature of the following verses, 20-22 (which are not resolved, i.e. the Greeks' request is neither granted nor denied, and the Greeks themselves disappear), which hardly constituted the continuation of the preceding pericope, but rather as a frgament are themselves used by John as an introduction to the discourse beginning in v. 23. John, then, used for his account of the entry into Jerusalem a fragmentary written source of the same type (liturgical or catechetical) that Luke did.

Finally, Luke's source, in attributing to Jesus before his entry into Jerusalem a multitude of disciples accompanying him near Jerusalem, as well as attributing to him a number of miracles which this crowd had witnessed, agrees with John's source (where the crowd of pilgrims who come to acclaim Jesus must have known much about him, or they would not have acclaimed him as Israel's king) and John's gospel (on this aspect of which see below, p. 110), in that all three recount or presuppose that Jesus was active in Jerusalem prior to the time of his triumphal entry—in this regard differing from the evangelists Mark, Matthew and Luke. On the basis of Mk. 10. 46-52, Lk. 13. 34 f. (cf. Mt. 23. 37 ff.), and the behaviour of Joseph of Arimathea in burying Jesus, all of which support a view of Jesus as present in Jerusalem for more than a few days at the end of his life, we may say that it is likely that Luke's and John's sources here, along with John's general picture, are on this point to be preferred to Mark and Matthew—that is to say that the scheme of a single journey of Jesus to Jerusalem at the end of his ministry was adopted by Mark not on the basis of historical tradition but in order to make his account simpler and more coherent.

We conclude, then, that Luke and John each had a written non-Marcan source at this point, that neither source was more than an isolated frgament, that both are historically reliable insofar as they presuppose Jesus as having already been active in Jerusalem, and that Luke's source presupposes an account of Jesus' movements such as we find not in Luke's but in John's gospel. It is not possible at this point to evaluate the significance of this last fact; that we can do only after we have analyzed the further points on which Luke and John agree.

CHAPTER SIX

SATAN AND JUDAS

Luke 22. 3 / John 13. 2, 27a

Both Luke (22. 3) and John (13. 27a) contain statements that Satan entered into Judas Iscariot, though Luke has this statement in connection with his account of Judas' plot with the chiefpriests, which he recounts just before the account of the preparation for the Passover/last supper, whereas John says that Satan entered into Judas after Jesus gave him a morsel in the course of the last supper. The two statements are virtually identical: Luke has εἰσῆλθεν δὲ σατανᾶς εἰς 'Ιούδαν κτλ. whereas John reads καὶ μετὰ τὸ ψωμίον τότε εἰσῆλθεν εἰς ἐκεῖνον ὁ σατανᾶς.

Before we attempt to explain this agreement, we must take into account Jn. 13. 2, which in connection with the last supper also contains a statement concerning the devil and Judas. Just after the statement that a meal (i.e. the last supper) was occurring, the Egyptian manuscripts and the Vulgate offer the text: τοῦ διαβόλου ἤδη βεβληκότος εἰς τὴν καρδίαν ἵνα παραδοῖ αὐτὸν 'Ιούδας Σίμωνος Ισκαριώτης. [1] Two meanings for this are advanced: ". . . . the devil already having put it into the heart of Judas Iscariot, Simon's son, to beray him (i.e. Jesus) . . . ." [2] and ". . . the devil having already resolved in his heart that Judas Iscariot Simon's son should betray him." [3] Bauer [4] defends the first meaning on the ground that Judas' name is put at the end for emphasis. If one accepted this reading, then it would be true that both 13. 2 and 13. 27 would be close parallels to Lk. 22. 3, the first parallel not only as to what occurred, but as to when (i.e. shortly before the last supper), the second recounting the same occurrence in the same words, but placing it later in the sequence of events. But despite Bauer's observation, his interpretation is syntactically very difficult, and in addition it produces a reading for Jn. 13. 2 which conflicts with

---

[1] This is the original reading, as is shown on p. 30, nt. 2.

[2] So—following Origen—Bauer, Lagrange and Wikenhauser in their commentaries, Zurhellen, *op. cit.*, p. 52, and the Revised Standard Version.

[3] So Barrett, *op. cit.*, *ad loc.*, and the Zürich German translation.

[4] Bauer, *op. cit.*, *ad loc.*

13. 27 as to when Satan entered into Jesus. [1] In view of the parallels which Barrett is able to offer for the second reading (e.g. Lk. 21. 14, Job 22. 22 LXX, 1 Sam. 29. 10 LXX), it is to be preferred. [2]

We have with Lk. 22. 3, Jn. 13. 2 and Jn. 13. 27 an interesting phenomenon. John presents two statements, both of which in differing ways are parallel to a statement in Luke, though Jn. 13. 2 is not so close a one according to the reading we've adopted as it is according to the other. As far as the Jn. 13. 27 statement is concerned, there is no question that John derived it from Luke. As we have seen, John knew Luke's gospel; that he drew on it here is ensured by his use of the Lucan σατανᾶς, [3] a use which indicates that he was so struck by Luke's statement that the wording of it remained in his mind. [4] He did not, however, follow Luke in every regard even here; rather, he meditated on Luke's statement, and in

---

[1] A number of commentators who accept a reading for Jn. 13. 2 which puts it in conflict with 13. 27 solve the problem by deleting one or the other as a late gloss. So Bultmann, *op. cit.*, because he sees v. 2 as overfilled with genitive absolutes, strikes out that part of it which concerns us as a late addition. Zurhellen, *op. cit.*, p. 52, because he sees μετὰ τὸ ψωμίον in v. 27 as a doublet of λαβὼν οὖν τὸ ψωμίον (v. 30), and because of the close verbal similarity of v. 27 to Lk 22. 3, regards v. 27a as an insertion into John's text from Luke. In support of this can be advanced the fact that of the six times John refers to the devil, only here is he called σατανᾶς (in 8. 44 and 13. 2 he is called ὁ διάβολος, in 12. 31, 14. 20 and 16. 11 ὁ ἄρχων τοῦ κόσμου τούτου or ὁ τοῦ κόσμου ἄρχων), whereas in Luke this appelation appears five times. But there is no more manuscript support for Zurhellen's postulation than there is for Bultmann's. It is of course possible that before the gospel was copied in the form from which all our manuscripts spring, it had already undergone various revisions. But, except as concerns Jn. 21, the various efforts to distinguish these disagree so radically with one another that the rôle that subjectivity plays in such efforts is apparent, which should discourage too prodigal a revising of the text on the basis of the unevenness in it which does undoubtedly exist. This unevenness is, as Albertz, *Die Botschaft des Neuen Testaments*, I/1, pp. 246 f. points out, probably in large measure due to the fact that the evangelist when he wrote was a very old man.

[2] Bultmann, *op. cit.*, p. 353, nt. 4, champions for 13. 2 the text of the *Koine*, D, Koridethi and some of the Old Latin and the Syrian translations, which gives with unobjectionable syntax the same reading which Bauer, etc. advance for the ℵ text. But this reading is clearly an attempt to smooth the other, and so secondary. Bultmann's grounds for preferring it are that both meanings advanced for the other, i. e. the ℵ text, are impossible. Barrett's he excludes on the count that in that case, according to the expression βάλλεσθαι εἰς νοῦν, the middle voice, βεβλημένου, not βεβληκότος, would have had to be used. Here, however, we have an expression containing not νοῦς but καρδία.

[3] For the statistics see nt. 1 above.

[4] As to the statement in Luke, it is found in the middle of a section (21. 1-13) where he is following Mark very closely, which justifies us in the

taking it over he altered its position and expanded it. He located it not where Luke did, but in the course of the last supper, after Jesus, having told the disciples that one of them will betray him and having said to the beloved disciple that it will be he to whom he gives a morsel, gives the morsel to Judas. John clearly thought that this location, stressing as it did Jesus' mastery of the situation, and possibly making an oblique point similar to that of 1 Cor. 11. 29, was more fitting than Luke's. [1] Nevertheless, he was also impressed by the location of Luke's statement, providing as it does part of the framework for the account of the last supper. He therefore inserted at the corresponding point in his gospel (i.e. at 13. 2) a statement which he composed on the basis of his meditation on Lk. 22. 3 and which, in that it prepared the reader of the gospel for 13. 25, he used to reinforce that statement. [2]

We may summarize our findings by saying that the tradition attributing Judas' betrayal to the inspiration of the devil entered the gospel tradition through the activity of the third evangelist, and was taken over and elaborated by John.

---

view that the evangelist inserted it here, deriving it from an orally circulating tradition or possibly (see nt. 2 below) from his own theological reflection.

[1] J. H. Holtzmann, *op. cit.*, p. 73, correctly points out that this alteration in chronology constitutes a correction of Luke. But this fact is of less significance than the fact that John has here drawn on Luke.

[2] The two statements in John and the one in Luke contribute to theological formulations which are different in each gospel. In Luke (see on this Conzelmann, *op. cit.*, p. 135), Jesus' ministry consists of two periods in which Satan (and temptation) are present for Jesus and his disciples, i. e. the beginning (4. 1-13) and the end (from 22. 3 on, particularly vv. 22. 28, 31, 40, 53 b), with a period characterized by the absence of both Satan and temptation in between. In John, on the other hand, Jesus' passion is the time of the devil's presence (so 13. 27, 14. 30), and the time of his downfall (12. 31, 16. 11). (In Lk. 10. 18 we have, it is true, a passage analogous to Jn. 12. 31, but in Luke the fall of Satan occurs during the ministry of Jesus and the seventy, and is not specifically related to the passion.)

Luke and John agree, however, in associating Satan with Judas, whereas in Mark (8. 33) and, following him, Matthew (16. 23), he is associated with Peter. Though it is true that Luke suppressed Mk. 8. 33 as part of his effort to spare the disciples wherever possible (he did, however, in 22. 31 bring a tradition which is probably, though very distantly, related to Mk. 8. 33), it is not true, as Lightfoot, *History and Interpretation in the Gospels*, p. 172, maintains, that Luke and John in their statements about the devil and Judas sought primarily to excuse Judas, as one of the twelve, for his betrayal on the count that he was at that point possessed by the devil. Rather we have evidence here of theological reflection on the scandalous fact of Judas' betrayal and on the nature of the forces which opposed Jesus, reflection which lead to the view that these forces at root were not human but demonic.

CHAPTER SEVEN

THE LAST SUPPER

Luke 22. 14-38 / John 13-17

We come now to Luke's and John's accounts of the last supper. [1] We may by way of a preliminary remark say that Luke's account agrees with Mark's and Matthew's in recounting the institution of

[1] We have already examined the Lk. 22. 3/Jn. 13. 29a parallel (where the Johannine verse falls within the last supper account, but the Lucan verse precedes it) because we found it convenient in the course of the monograph to discuss Lucan-Johannine parallels in the order in which they appear in Luke.

Here should be mentioned an assertion of Gaussen (*op. cit.*, p. 568), Osty ("Les Points de Contact Entre Le Recit de la Passion Dans Saint Luc et Saint Jean," *Mélanges Jules Lebreton, Recherches de Science Religieuse*, 1951, p. 154) and Foster ("Go and make ready," *Expository Times*, 1952, p. 193) that Peter and John appear together in Lk. 22. 8 and Jn. 13. 24, and further in Acts 3. 1-4. 23, 8. 14-25 and Jn. 21. 7 f., 10-23. Osty concludes from this that both evangelists like to show Peter and John together. These assertions depend on the identification of the beloved disciple of the fourth gospel with John the son of Zebedee, for it is the beloved disciple whom the fourth evangelist mentions as together with Peter in the aforementioned places in his gospel; neither there nor anywhere else (except 21. 2) does he mention John the son of Zebedee by name. Two very strong arguments militate, however, against this identification. (a) If the beloved disciple had been John the son of Zebedee, and the fourth gospel had been written with him as guarantor of its authority (for that the beloved disciple himself wrote the gospel, i. e. that it was written by an eyewitness of the events described, is, despite καὶ ὁ γράψας ταῦτα in 21. 24, excluded by—to name but one of many considerations—the evangelist's use of Mark and Luke and other sources, which if he had been an eyewitness would have been unnecessary), it would not have lacked an account of the transfiguration, at which John the son of Zebedee was present. (b) John the son of Zebedee, as we know from Gal. 2. 9, was one of the leaders of the Jerusalem Jewish-Christian party, whose theology, from what Paul tells us of it, was in the sharpest conflict with the theology of the fourth evangelist; it is hardly conceivable that the latter could have regarded a Jewish-Christian as the guarantor of the truth of his gospel. Here, in fact, lies the answer to the popular argument (advanced e.g. by Michaelis, *Einleitung in das Neue Testament*, p. 97) that it is no accident that John the son of Zebedee is never mentioned expressly in John except in ch. 21, because he is otherwise mentioned in the form of the beloved disciple. Rather he is never mentioned (except in 21. 2, where he is not mentioned by name but rather lumped together with his brother) implicitly or explicitly because the evangelist was opposed to the party of which, after Jesus' death and resurrection, he was one of the leaders. As to who the beloved disciple was—even though it is likely he was no purely ideal

the eucharist, whereas John's recounts instead Jesus' washing of the disciples' feet. Luke and John agree, however, in that both bring a group of words of Jesus in the scene which we may fairly call a last discourse. Because of it their accounts of the scene are longer than Mark's or Matthew's; whereas Mark's account comprises nine verses (14. 17-25) and Matthew's ten (26. 20-29), Luke's is twenty-five verses long (22. 14-38) and John's is one hundred fifty-four. [1] The difference between the length of Luke's last discourse and John's is manifest; in Luke, if one includes the prophecy of the betrayal, it comprises eighteen verses (22. 21-38); in John, where the betrayal prophecy is usually not included because the departure of Judas which follows it is considered to mark the discourse's beginning, it comprises ninety-nine verses (13. 31-16. 33) not counting the ch. 17 prayer. The result of this difference

---

figure invented by the evangelist, but rather represents his patron apostle—we cannot be certain. If the evangelist was a member of the Hellenist party within the Church—on which see below, pp. 111 f.—then it's possible the beloved disciple was one of Christ's immediate followers who was also a Hellenist. The name Philip comes to mind, as the only one of the twelve who had a Greek name, and so quite likely lived in a manner akin to that of the Hellenists, i.e. a non-Jewish manner; interestingly enough, John's gospel brings special traditions about Philip in 1. 44 ff., 6. 5 ff., 12. 21 f. and 14. 9 f. However, this identification is problematical, for why would the evangelist sometimes call the person in question Philip and sometimes the beloved disciple?

[1] This last figure presupposes the view that chs. 15-17 in John cannot be effectively detached from chs. 13-14 and labelled as not belonging to the last supper scene. If one takes both Jn. 14. 31 b and 18. 1 at face value, then chs. 15-17, including the prayer in ch. 17, must be understood as having been spoken by Jesus while walking through the narrow streets of Jerusalem. But in the synoptic parallels to Jn. 18. 1 (Mk. 14. 26, Mt. 26. 30, Lk. 22. 39) ἐξέρχεσθαι refers to the departure from the buildings where the supper took place; in view of the nature of Jn. 14-17, it is likely that ἐξέρχεσθαι in 18. 1 means the same thing. It appears (as Bauer, *Das Johannesevangelium*, p. 189, maintains) that chs. 15-17 were later inserted by the evangelist into his gospel, but not as material developing that of chs. 13 f., but rather material parallel to it. This explains the fact that, though chs. 15 f. contain many parallels to chs. 13 f. (for a list of these, see *ibid.*) some of these point to the priority of chs. 13 f. over chs. 15 f., some give the opposite impression. When chs. 15-17 were added, the evangelist overlooked 14. 31, which had made excellent sense when it immediately preceded 18. 1, but now no longer did. The efforts of commentators like Bernard, who incorporates chs. 14-16 into chs. 13 and 17, or Bultmann, who incorporates chs. 15-17 into chs. 13 f., suffer from the lack of objective evidence, which lack is evident in the fact that such efforts produce such radically varying results. At any event, they come to the same conclusion as far as our present purpose is concerned, i.e. that chs. 13-17 in their present form constitute a single scene, that of the last supper.

of length is that the institution of the eucharist not the words following on it dominates the scene in Luke, whereas in John the footwashing is dominated by the following discourse. Luke's last discourse comprises five units, the prophecy of the betrayal (22. 21-23), the rebuke to the disciples following on their quarrel (22. 24-27), the praise of and promise to the disciples (22. 28-30), the prophecy of Peter's denial (22. 31-34) and the words comparing the past and the future (22. 35-38). Of these, the second and fourth contain material closely parallel to material found in the Johannine last supper account. These parallels we shall now examine. [1]

In his rebuke to the disciples following on their dispute as to rank, Jesus points to himself (in Lk. 22. 26 f.) as one who serves, and enjoins the disciples to do likewise. In Jn. 13. 12b-16, Jesus does the same thing. To be sure, the word διακονεῖν does not appear in John's account, which bears no verbal resemblance to Luke's; but Jesus' words in John point to his immediately preceding footwashing, which is an act of διακονία. [2] From where did the

[1] We may here mention two unsuccessful attempts to demonstrate that elements in Luke's account of the last supper agree with John's gospel in dating the last supper, trial and crucifixion of Jesus on the 14th and not the 15th Nisan. Zimmermann, "Lukas und die johanneische Tradition," *Studien und Kritiken*, 1903, pp. 586-605, accepts the reading of D it sy, ἡ ἡμέρα τοῦ πάσχα, for Lk. 22. 7, and interprets the verse to mean that the Passover was coming, but had not yet arrived. He cites in support the contention of Chwolson, *Das letzte Passamahl Christi und der Tag seines Todes*, St. Petersburg 1892, pp. 37-44, that, when the Passover fell on the day before the Sabbath, then the slaying of the Passover lambs (Lk. 22. 7b) must be moved ahead a day, in order to avoid possible infraction of the Sabbath laws. But the aorist ἦλθον in 22. 7a precludes a meaning which would require the imperfect ἤρχετο; moreover, Schürer, *Theologische Literaturzeitung*, 1893, col. 82, points out the fallacy of assuming that the Sabbath (to say nothing of the day before the Sabbath) would take precedence over the Passover as regards observance of the law.

A second effort is that of Burkitt and A. E. Brooke, *Journal of Theological Studies*, 1908 pp. 569-572. They interpret 22. 15, "I have earnestly desired to eat this Passover with you before I suffer," to mean that Jesus is here expressing his realization that he won't be able to eat the Passover with his disciples as he had hoped, for he will no longer be alive. (Taylor, *op. cit.*, p. 7, follows Burkitt and Brook here, and thinks that not only 22. 15 but also 22. 16 makes this point). But this meaning for 22. 15 is excluded by οὐκέτι in the following verse. In fact, as far as the dating of Christ's death is concerned, Luke is no nearer John than are Mark and Matthew.

[2] The fact that the word διακονεῖν does not appear in John 13 may not be understood (with Zurhellen, *op. cit.*, p. 53) as indicating that Luke and John have in reality no common element here. The original meaning of διακονεῖν is 'to wait on, to serve at table', and, in contrast to all other Greek words denoting service, it emphasizes the personal nature of the service performed,

evangelists derive these passages? To answer this question for Luke, we must begin with an examination of the passage of which it forms a part, vv. 24-27. Of these four verses, the middle two are so close to Mk. 10. 42b-44 (despite the difference to which Klostermann [1] points, that whereas Mark in vv. 43 f. says that service is the way to greatness, Luke in v. 26 enjoins *noblesse oblige* on those who are outstanding) that it is natural to assume that he drew here on Mark. This assumption is confirmed by the fact that the preceding verse in Luke, v. 24, is very much like 9. 46; [2] this similarity speaks for both v. 24 and 9. 46 as stemming from the evangelist. It is confirmed also by the fact that 22. 24-27 does not fit well into its context; it is hard to conceive of a quarrel of the disciples as to rank following on the institution of the eucharist and the prophecy of the betrayal which caused such a shocked reaction (v. 23) on their part; in fact, this quarrel had no connection with the last supper until Luke transferred it from its position in Mark to its present one, for a reason we shall mention below. Luke drew on Mk. 10. 42b-44 for vv. 25 f., and composed v. 24 as an introduction. For Mk. 10. 45b he substituted the verse which concerns us, 22. 27: τίς γὰρ μείζων, ὁ ἀνακείμενος ἢ ὁ διακονῶν; οὐχὶ ὁ ἀνακείμενος; ἐγὼ δὲ ἐν μέσῳ ὑμῶν ὡς ὁ διακονῶν. [3] Here, as the presence of ἀνακεῖμαι

and the character of the service as a service of love (so Bayer, in *Theologisches Wörterbuch zum Neuen Testament*, ed. G. Kittel, II, p. 81). It is therefore clear that Jesus' act in Jn. 13, performed at table, constitutes one of διακονία in the narrowest sense (*ibid*, p. 84). Vv. 13. 6-11, to be sure, contain an interpretation of this act which gives it quite another character than that of an example of διακονία; but in vv. 12-17 the latter interpretation occurs, and Wellhausen (*Das Evangelium Johannis, ad loc.*) and Bultmann (*op. cit., ad loc.*), who correctly distinguish two strata here, agree that 12. 17, as that offering the simpler and clearer interpretation, is the earlier.

[1] Klostermann, *Das Lukasevangelium, ad loc.*

[2] Cf. especially the second half of both verses.

[3] D, unsupported by other mss., offers a variant here and in the following verse. But, as Bayer, *op. cit.*, p. 84, points out, aside from the weak support for this reading, the absense of the vivid contrast between the prevailing concept of the better position and Jesus' own concept, and the presence of a didactic sentence concerning the disciples, indicate its secondary character. Cadbury, *Making of Luke-Acts*, p. 280 and nt., on the basis of the emphasis in the speeches of Acts on Christ's resurrection rather than his death, and of the fact that where Luke does quote Isa. 53 (in Acts 8. 32 f.) he quotes none of the substitutionary atonement phrases, postulates a lack of interest on Luke's part in the effect of Christ's death, and in this context mentions Luke's failure to include Mk. 10. 45 b in his gospel. There may be something in this, but the thesis loses much of its force if one accepts (see p. 18, nt. 2) 22. 19b-20, with its emphasis on the atoning aspects of Christ's death, as part of Luke's original text.

shows, διακονεῖν still has its original meaning of "to wait on, to serve at table." [1] Jesus says that he is amongst the disciples as he who serves at table. But where in Luke's gospel is it recorded that Jesus served at table? Wellhausen [2] and Manson [3] regard Jesus' actions at the last supper as a serving at table. But Jesus there has acted as the head of a household celebrating the Passover feast; his distribution of the bread and wine is an act of authority not of table service. [4] Plummer and Klostermann [5] deny that the statement refers to a specific act, regarding it as having the character of a parable, a parable pointing to Jesus' whole life as one of service; but the fact that Luke deleted Mk. 10. 45, where διακονῆσαι does refer to Jesus' life as whole, and introduced instead a verse with phraseology of a concreteness absent in the Marcan verse, makes this unlikely.

In fact, Lk. 22. 27 presupposes a concrete action on Jesus' part which not he but John records. [6] Why, without recording the act to which it points, has Luke placed it here—and as part of an account of a quarrel of the disciples which also doesn't fit here well? Before attempting to answer this let us look at the situation in John. The classical critical view is that John spun the whole of 13. 1-17 out of Lk. 22. 27. [7] But this is disproved by the presence in vv. 6-17 of two conflicting interpretations of the significance of the footwashing. [8] Both cannot have stemmed from the evangelist; rather he found the footwashing and the first interpretation (that in vv. 6-11) in a written source, and added the second (12-17) himself. [9] Therewith we are in a position to answer

---

[1] So both Bauer, *Wörterbuch zum Neuen Testament, ad loc.*, and Bayer, *op. cit.*, pp. 83, 85. In this it differs from Mk. 10. 45, where διακονεῖν has the general meaning of "service" and is focused on Christ's redeeming death (v. 45b).

[2] Wellhausen, *Das Evangelium Lucae, ad loc.*

[3] Manson, Wm. *The Gospel of Luke, ad loc.*

[4] So correctly Zahn and Klostermann in their commentaries.

[5] In their commentaries, *ad loc.*

[6] This remains the case even if, as Zurhellen, *op. cit.*, p. 53 and Reicke, *Diakonie, Festfreude und Zelos*, pp. 30 f., maintain, διακονεῖν in 22. 26 has liturgical connotations.

[7] This view is held by Strauss, *The Life of Jesus*, p. 625, Windisch, *op. cit.*, p. 51, Bultmann, *Die Geschichte der synoptischen Tradition*, p. 49, and Creed, *op. cit.*, p. 320. However, even among radical critics, it is not universally held, e.g. Zurhellen, *op. cit.*, p. 53, and Grant, *op. cit.*, p. 293.

[8] See p. 34, nt. 2.

[9] In the absence of any verbal similarity between vv. 12-17 and Lk 22. 26f., there is no reason whatever to think John drew on Luke here. Why would he,

the question asked above about Luke. The evidence points to a tradition circulating to the effect that Jesus washed the feet of his disciples at the last supper. This came to John in written form, and he incorporated it into his gospel, giving it the position occupied in the synoptic gospels by the institution of the eucharist—which last he dealt with elsewhere (6. 51-58). Luke, on the other hand, writing somewhat earlier, knew a similar tradition, apparently still circulating in oral form. [1] He was unwilling to use it in its full form because it might appear to compete with, and so detract from, the institution of the eucharist. Still, he wanted to include some reference to it in his gospel, and realized that if he inserted such a reference where the event itself belonged, i.e. in the account of the last supper, it could be one of a group of words of Jesus which he wished to put there. He therefore combined it with Mk. 10. 42b-44 and put it where he did, despite the unevenness which resulted. [2]

Luke and John, departing from Matthew and Mark, both record Jesus' prediction of Peter's denial (Lk. 22. 31-34, Jn. 13. 36-38) as occurring during the last supper. Before discussing this and related chronological agreements, it will be convenient to analyze certain agreements within the two pericopes and between the Lucan pericope and material found elsewhere in John's gospel. In Luke (22. 34) Jesus says λέγω σοι, Πέτρε, οὐ φωνήσει σήμερον ἀλέκτωρ ἕως τρίς με ἀπαρνήσῃ μὴ εἰδέναι, in John (13. 38) ἀμὴν ἀμὴν λέγω σοι, οὐ μὴ ἀλέκτωρ φωνήσῃ ἕως οὗ ἀρνήσῃ με τρίς. Mark on the other hand reads ἀμὴν λέγω σοι ὅτι σὺ σήμερον ταύτῃ τῇ νυκτὶ πρὶν ἢ δίς ἀλέκτορα φωνῆσαι τρίς με ἀπαρνήσῃ and Matthew, following him, differs little. Luke's and John's sentences have an οὐ . . . ἕως construction, whereas Matthew and Mark have a construction with πρίν which produces

whose purpose was to elucidate a passage he had just inserted into his gospel, draw on a fragmentary reference to the footwashing in Luke? Actually, in vv. 13-16, he drew on a variant of a Q saying (cf. Mk. 10. 24, Lk. 6. 40), a variant in part identical with an expansion of that saying found in Matthew but not in Luke.

[1] He also knew a related one which he used in Lk. 12. 37.

[2] As to whether the footwashing actually occurred at the last supper, it is impossible with certainty to say. The silence of Mark and Matthew is the strongest argument against its having done so. Yet it is likely that their silence, like Luke's partial silence, is due to a desire to focus attention at the last supper on the institution of the eucharist; as we shall see, Mark (and following him Matthew) in similar fashion has altered the sequence of events in order to produce a more fitting context for the institution. And the footwashing, in the way in which by means of it Jesus makes a point in startling and graphic fashion, rings very true to what we know of him.

an entirely different sentence syntactically, though the vocabulary is largely the same. Also, neither Luke nor John have the words ταύτῇ τῇ νυκτί which appear in Mark and Matthew. [1] There are, too, similarities between the structure of the Lucan and Johannine pericopes. In both, Peter gives only one assurance of his steadfastness (and that one an assurance to the death), [2] which directly precedes Jesus' prophecy, and the prophecy concludes the pericope. In Mark and Matthew, Jesus' prophecy if fitted in between two different assurances of Peter's, only the second of which mentions a readiness to die. Lastly, a thematic similarity may be mentioned. In both Luke (v. 32: "when you have turned back, strengthen your brothers") and John (v. 36: "you will follow later"—i.e. to the Father: cf. 14. 2) the prophecy of Peter's denial entails a prophecy of, or (in John) implies, his eventual persistence in the faith. [3]

The differences between Luke and John here are, however, considerable. In Luke, Peter's assurance of steadfastness is made in response to a statement of Jesus about Satan, himself and Peter (v. 31 f.) which only Luke brings. [4] In John, Peter's statement is

[1] κύριε, which appears in Lk. 22. 33 (in Peter's statement of loyalty) and in many mss. in Jn. 13. 37 (in Peter's question which precedes his statement of loyalty), is too common a form of address for Jesus in Luke (where it appears about twenty times as against once in Mark) and John (where it appears almost thirty times) to be a significant parallel in otherwise entirely differing sentences.

[2] Bultmann, *Das Evangelium des Johannes*, *ad loc.*, interprets τίθημι τὴν ψυχήν in Jn. 13. 28 to mean not "lay down", but "risk one's life," but the LXX passages which he cites in support, Judg. 12. 3 and 1 Kgs. 19. 5, contain the words ἐν τῇ χειρί μου (σου), which are here lacking, and this interpretation is by no means necessary in Jn. 10. 11, as he maintains it is. Actually, the difference in meaning is slight.

[3] Indeed, this phrase in John (. . . . ἀκολουθήσεις ὕστερον) probably, analogous to ἀκολούθει in 21. 19, refers to Peter's martyrdom. If, as Rengstorf, *op. cit.*, *ad loc.*, maintains, Luke added "to prison" to Peter's v. 32 oath in view of Acts 4 and 12, then he probably understood "to death" in the same verse in similarly concrete fashion, so that in his account too we have an —unwitting—reference by Peter to his future martyrdom.

[4] V. 33 undeniably represents a response to vv. 31 f. in the present gospel. However, the odd composition of vv. 31-34 has often been noted, in which the positive content of 31 f. (Jesus' intercessory prayer overcoming Satan's opposition, and his commission of Jesus) is followed by vv. 33 f. with their negative content, i. e. the prediction of the denial. (Because of this, it is impossible to determine whether Peter's response in v. 33 is one of protest, in line with the ἐπιστρέψας of v. 32, or of proud affirmation, in tune with the remaining content of vv. 31 f.) This confusing reversal in vv. 31-34 of the internal development we'd expect, plus the fact that Jesus calls the

preceded by a question of his in response to a statement of Jesus that Peter will follow, but only later (vv. 36-37a), which altercation is special to John; and Jesus (as is not the case in Luke) repeats Peter's declaration of faithfulness before he predicts his denial. Moreover, the references to Peter's persistence in the faith and martyrdom are expressed in entirely different terms.

What are we to conclude about the connection of Luke and John here? That they had a common written source from which they derived the οὐ . . . ἕως construction? Luke, to be sure, had for vv. 33 f. (which, as we saw in nt. 4, he combined with vv. 31 f.) a written source, as the occurrence in v. 34 of the completely un-Lucan address form Πέτρε shows.[1] Did John draw on the same source? Against his having done so militates the lack of similarity between Luke's and John's accounts as regards the phrases in which Peter maintains his loyalty. Did John compose his whole passage himself, and is the similarity to Luke purely accidental? No, for ἕως with an aorist subjunctive, though it is a very common construction in the New Testament, occurs only this once in John. The evidence points, rather, to John's having been struck by the dramatic way in which Jesus' prophecy forms the conclusion of Luke's pericope, and by the wording of that prophecy. He therefore used both in his account, though he cast vv. 36-37a in terms of the context into which he fitted the incident, i.e. Jesus' statement in v. 33 that where he is going the disciples cannot come. As to John's reference to Peter's martyrdom, it may be that he derived it from Luke, though expressing it in entirely different terms—but it may be that John, whose theological interests in the last discourse ran strongly in the direction of stressing the positive aspects of the situation,[2] here independently of Luke mentioned the ultimate, faithful stage of Peter's life.[3]

We must now examine two elements in Lk. 22. 31-34 which have parallels in Johannine material found in other parts of the fourth gospel. In Lk. 22. 32, Jesus states that he has prayed

disciple Σίμων in v. 31 and Πέτρος in v. 34, point to vv. 31 f. and vv. 33 f. as having been separate until joined together by Luke.

[1] So correctly Plummer, *op. cit.*, *ad loc.*, who disagrees with Bultmann, *op. cit.*, p. 287 f.

[2] See p. 45, nt. 2.

[3] Grant (*op. cit.*, p. 296) maintains that Jn. 13. 36-38 does not draw on Luke but bases his account on Mk. 14. 27-31. There is, however, aside from the occurrence of ἀμήν in both Mk. 14. 30 and Jn. 13. 38, no evidence to support this view.

that Peter's faith may not fail. In view of the preceding verse, it is clear that the content of this prayer is that God might protect Peter against Satan, who has asked from God (and, apparently, received) permission to test him. In Jn. 17. 15, in the course of the highpriestly prayer, Jesus asks God to protect the faithful ἐκ τοῦ πονηροῦ. This adjectival noun can be interpreted either in a masculine ('from the evil one') or neuter ('from evil') sense. That the former is correct, though John's gospel offers no directly parallel use of ὁ πονηρός, is clear from Jn. 12. 31, 13. 27, 14. 30 and 16. 11, which make the evangelist's belief in the devil amply clear, plus the occurrence of ὁ πονηρός for the devil in 1 Jn. 2. 13 f., 3. 12 and 5. 18.[1] The striking similarity of this to Lk. 22. 32 is evident. How can it be explained?

With the exception of the Catholics (except for Wikenhauser) and of Bernard, modern commentators are agreed that the hand of the evangelist is responsible for the form and extent of the prayer, and for much or all of its content. The former is confirmed for 17. 15 by the occurrence in it of the combination ἀλλ' ἵνα, which never appears in Matthew and Mark, only once in Luke, and in all eleven times in the fourth gospel. As for John's last discourse, Hoskyns[2] cautions against a view which sees the evangelist as having no interest in the historical situation,[3] and 17. 15 proves he's right. For the most natural explanation of it[4] is that John in reading Luke had encountered the tradition of Jesus' praying for God's protection of Peter against Satan located in the account of the last supper, and had reflected on it, the result being 17. 15. The fact that John used elements from Lk. 22. 31-34 at two widely disparate points in the last discourse shows the freedom with which he worked.

Finally, there is a correspondence between Jesus' command to Peter in 22. 32b "when you've turned back, strengthen your brothers" and Jesus' threefold command to Peter, "feed my lambs (sheep)," in Jn. 21. 15-17. The simplest explanation for the repetition of the latter command (and Peter's answer "I love you") is

---

[1] So virtually all the modern commentators except Bernard, *op. cit.*, *ad loc.* (who in this respect follows Augustine and Chrysostum), and Bultmann, *op. cit.*, *ad loc.*, who reserves judgment.

[2] Hoskyns, *The Fourth Gospel*, *ad loc.*

[3] So Bauer and Barrett in their commentaries, *ad loc.*

[4] Surely more convincing than the view that we have here two independent traditions of the same word of Jesus.

that we have here a conscious correspondence to Peter's threefold denial [1]—by which we see that both commissions to Peter occur in passages related to his denial, the one predicting it, the other reinstating Peter after it. This is not the only correspondence between Lk. 22. 31-34 and Jn. 15. 15-19. In Lk. 22. 33 Peter affirms his loyalty towards Jesus, in Jn. 22. 15, 16, 17 he affirms his love. Further, Peter's 22. 23 statement entails, in its present form, a reference to the martyrdom he was to suffer—as does Jesus' statement in 21. 18. There are so many correspondences here that it's clear the two passages must somehow be related. [2] However, the correspondences are found in passages within differing frameworks, in Luke that of the last supper discourse, in John that of a resurrection scene. To postulate that John on the basis of Lk. 22. 31-34 and a knowledge of how Peter died, constructed 21. 15-19 in order to provide a foil for what he has to say about the beloved disciple in vv. 20-24 is to assume a great deal in the name of John's sense of his pneumatic authority, but it is nevertheless possible that this is what happened. Still, in view of the fact that we know from 1 Cor. 15. 5 and Lk. 24. 34 that Christ did indeed appear to an unaccompanied Peter, and that Jn. 21. 15-19 is the only resurrection appearance described in any gospel points to that event, it is better to see here a tradition which, quite probably having no connection with Galilee, John found before him, and added to 21. 1-14. [3] As for Lk. 22. 31-34, it is clear that vv. 33-34 belong where they are. This is, however, not true of vv. 31 f. If, as we saw above, the evangelist joined vv. 31 f. to vv. 33 f. in fashioning his account of the last supper, then we must reckon with the possibility that vv. 31 f. did not belong in the last supper scene until Luke put them there. [4] The only word in the two verses which firmly roots

---

[1] Bultmann, *op. cit.*, *ad loc.*, denies reference here to Peter's denial, but this indicates a failure to do justice to the otherwise inexplicable fact of repetition.

[2] So Cullmann, *Peter*, p. 183, and Bultmann, *op. cit.*, *ad loc.*

[3] The only words connecting vv. 15-18 with vv. 1-14 are ὅτε οὖν ἠρίστησαν and πλέον τούτων in v. 15, and these will have been added by John in connecting the two.

[4] That Luke did not compose vv. 31 f. himself is (so Bultmann, *Geschichte der synoptischen Tradition*, p. 287, and Klostermann, *op. cit.*, *ad loc.*) clear from the fact that v. 32 b presupposes the flight of the disciples, an event Luke doesn't record. v. 32 b must have already been connected with vv. 30-31a when Luke encountered it, and Luke incorporated the two verses into his gospel without taking cognizance of it.

them where they are is ἐπιστρέψας, if this is understood as having the meaning 'having turned (back)', which then clearly points to the imminent denial.[1] A possible explanation of the present position of vv. 31 ff., here advanced as the best one, is that originally they figured as part of a resurrection appearance, in which Peter's denial, as in Jn. 21. 15-19, is looked back upon; this explains the positive tone of the two verses which has been noted. When Luke, who perhaps already found these verses detached from their original setting, connected them with vv. 33 f., he added ἐπιστρέψας to weld the two parts together.[2] In Lk. 22. 31 f. and Jn. 21. 15-17 we have two variant traditions of a resurrection appearance to Peter, though they are not verbally close enough to one another to justify the view that one is directly dependent on the other.[3]

Having discussed all the agreements between specific verses in Luke's and John's accounts of the last supper, we must now mention a remarkable agreement between the two as to the sequence of the events comprising the last supper scene. In both gospels that sequence is: (a) sacramental act (i.e. in Luke the institution of the eucharist, in John the footwashing),[4] (b) prophecy of Judas' betrayal, (c) prophecy of Peter's denial, (d) end of the scene. In Mark the sequence, on the other hand, is b-a-d-c: prophecy of

---

[1] ἐπιστρέψας can be understood in two other senses. It can, as a Hebraism, mean "in turn," as in the LXX text of Ps. 85. 7. (Manson, *op. cit.*, *ad loc.*, following Maldonatus, Grotius and Bengel, advocates this meaning for Luke here.) Or it can, taken transitively, mean ,,cause to turn," producing the reading "you, after you've converted your brethren, strengthen them." In either case, there would originally have been no reference to Peter's denial, though such a reference would have been seen, after he fastened the two verses to the account of the prediction of the denial, by both the evangelist and his readers. However, in view of the fact that ἐπιστρέψας is found in Acts eight times, and always with an intransitive sense, as a technical missionary term meaning "turn (towards the Lord)," it is probable that it has this meaning here, and that it is attributable to the evangelist.

[2] So Bultmann and Schmid in their commentaries, neither of whom, however, states where vv. 31 f. originally belonged.

[3] But cf. Oscar Cullmann, whose view (*op. cit.*, pp. 182 f.) that Jn. 21. 15-19 is a replica of Lk. 22. 31-34, which attests to the latter and can only be understood in the light of it, points in the opposite direction. So too does his statement, *ibid.*, made partly on the basis of the parallels between Mk. 16. 17-19 and Jn. 21. 15-19, that Peter's confession (Mt. 16. 17-19) actually occurred in the course of the last supper, in the position to which Lk. 22. 31-34 points.

[4] That the footwashing had sacramental character in the evangelist's eyes is clear from vv. 6-11 (the interpretation of it which he added when incorporating vv. 4 f., 12-16 into his gospel).

Judas' betrayal, institution of the eucharist, end of scene, prophecy of Peter's denial (on the way to Gethsemane). How is this state of affairs to be explained? Luke in the last supper scene drew on various written sources, i.e. on Mark for his account of Jesus' prophecy of Judas' betrayal [1] and for vv. 25 f., on Q for vv. 28 ff., on another source for the institution of the eucharist, [2] on two different written fragments for Peter's denial, on further material for the discourse on the past and the future in vv. 35-38. [3] These sources are of so diverse a nature that we have no justification for seeing Luke here as having had a non-Marcan written source for the scene as a whole, or even for an extensive part of it. The different components of the scene were, rather, put together by Luke. Did the sequence of events, differing as it does from Mark's, originate in his mind? One consideration prevents us from assuming this. The scene in its present sequence presents a picture which in no way corresponds to the picture which a pious reconstruction would produce. The opening institution of the eucharist is followed by the prediction of Judas' betrayal—which sequence raises the problem of how, though Jesus knew of his coming betrayal, he could celebrate the eucharist with his disciples without making any reference to the breach in their fellowship which he knew existed. Also, the importance of the institution is somewhat neutralized by the subsequent predictions of Judas' betrayal and of Peter's denial and by the quarrel among the disciples.

The situation as regards Mark is entirely different. The prophecy of Judas' betrayal opens the scene and its effect is neutralized by the following institution; moreover, this order of events forestalls the question Luke's account raises as to why Jesus without referring to the betrayal celebrated the eucharist. Furthermore, the scene ends on the positive note of the eucharist; the prophecy of Peter's denial occurs only after the group has left the meal and is on its way to Gethsemane. The order of events in Mark's account gives every indication of being secondary as over against that in Luke. [4] There is every reason to think that the original sequence of

---

[1] That he here drew on Mark is clear from a comparison of 22. 22 with Mk. 14. 21. [2] See p. 18, nt. 2.

[3] Vv. 35-38 appear to have been pieced together by the evangelist from isolated statements (e.g. vv. 36, 38a and possibly 37) which he joined together (thereby determining the present meaning of v. 36), and to which he added v. 35 (cf. 10. 4) as an introduction.

[4] So Zahn, *Das Evangelium des Lucas, ad loc.*

events was still preserved in oral tradition at the time when Mark and Luke wrote their gospels, and that it was taken up into his gospel by Luke but not by Mark into his. [1] It is, moreover, likely that this oral tradition contained a reference to Jesus' footwashing, whence Luke derived his knowledge of it. [2] In this case it related the institution of the eucharist, the prophecy of Judas' betrayal, the footwashing and the prophecy of Peter's denial in that order—all as occurring in the course of the last supper.

Did John know this oral tradition? [3] The answer is that he did—though he did not derive his knowledge of the footwashing from that alone, for as we saw he had in addition a written source for the incident. On one important point he departed from this oral tradition; he transplanted treatment of the eucharist from here to ch. 6, and, giving the footwashing the importance in the scene which in the synoptics the institution of the eucharist has, he moved the former to the beginning of the scene. But the oral tradition was nevertheless of considerable importance to him, as the following point makes clear. John's last discourse begins in 13. 31, and John composed the third verse of it (13. 33) in such a way that it constitutes the occasion of the prophecy of Peter's denial in 13. 36-38. But, despite the freedom with which we see him working here, he adhered to the order of events as contained in the oral tradition in that he located the prophecy of Peter's denial not after the end of the scene, as in Mark, but before it, as in the oral tradition.

We have now analyzed all the close parallels which occur between particular passages in Luke's last supper account and in John's, [4]

---

[1] That Luke followed it rather than the less sombre Marcan account is probably to be explained on the basis of the fact that it accords better with his view of the last supper as ushering in the time of temptation for Jesus and for the Church—on which see Conzelmann, *op. cit.*, pp. 67 f.

[2] The reference to Jesus' praise of and promise to the disciples was, of course, not derived from this source but, derived from Q, was inserted by Luke into the scene, as was the complex vv. 35-38, though parts of the latter (on 36 see Cullmann, *The State in the New Testament*, pp. 31 ff.) may preserve words spoken by Jesus at the last supper.

[3] Clearly he did not derive the order of the two prophecies from Luke —for in Luke's account the quarrel of the disciples and Jesus' subsequent rebuke, and his praise of and promise to the disciples, intervene between the two.

[4] If one assumes (with all modern commentators with the tentative exception of Loisy) that Lk. 22. 37 is not to be understood literally, as applying to the need for arms in the next few hours (which would result in an

as well as the agreement in the order of events. A question remains to be asked in regard to the last discourses which both locate here. Is it pure coincidence that Luke and John, unlike Mark and Matthew, both record a last discourse in the course of the last supper? The answer is that it is not. The idea of a discourse at this juncture originates with Luke, who with the aid of material from Mark and Q and of several isolated fragments constructed a last discourse in 22. 21-38. [1] John possessed a written account of the footwashing, but, since this concerned an action of Jesus and only secondarily words of his arising out of that action there is no reason to see in it the core of a farewell discourse which John, independent of any external influence, extended. Rather does the evidence point to John as having gotten the idea of a discourse at the last supper from Luke. John's dependence on Luke in this regard, however, should not be overestimated, as is clear from the relative length of the farewell discourses in the two gospels, which points to John as having radically extended, and virtually transformed, Luke at this point. [2]

---

intolerable conflict with 22. 51), but rather that Christ is here speaking symbolically about the future time of the Church beginning with his own death, then the disciples' response to it indicates their failure to understand Jesus. In that case we have here a parallel to the disciples' misunderstanding of Jesus in John's last discourse (14. 5, 14. 8). However, since different statements of Jesus are misunderstood in the two gospels, and since the theme of the disciples' obtuseness occurs often enough throughout John where he's not following the other gospels (i. e. in 4. 27, 31-34, 6. 60, 9. 2), it's clear he didn't derive 14. 5 or 14. 8 from Luke, but that the theme was a standard component of early Christian tradition. Another parallel of a purely formal nature does not need to be extensively discussed, as there is no need to postulate more than similar theological interest on the part of the two evangelists to explain it, i. e. the combination of Jesus' praise of and promise to the disciples in Lk. 22. 28-30 and Jn. 16. 25-27.

[1] To be sure, the oral tradition Luke (and John) knew placed the two prophecies and the footwashing after the institution, and so in a sense provided the nucleus of a last discourse. But Luke, by introducing material from Mk. 10 and from Q, and that fragment we find in vv. 31 f., made the narrative into one dominated by words of Jesus and so gave it the character of a discourse. Luke did not originate the last discourse as such, that distinction lying with Mark in his construction of Mk. 13. What Luke did was locate the last discourse elsewhere than where it had been in Mark, and give it another, i. e. primarily non-apocalyptic, character. (To be sure Luke took up the material from Mk. 13 into his gospel, though altering it significantly—but it no longer has the character of a last discourse, that coming only afterwards.)

[2] This transformation is graphically illustrated by the following point. For the third evangelist the discourse is the occasion for Jesus in vv. 35 f.,

Therewith our analysis of Luke's and John's last supper accounts is completed. We have determined that Luke and John both drew on pre-Marcan, probably historically accurate oral tradition for the order of events at the last supper, from which oral tradition Luke derived his knowledge of the footwashing. We further saw that John both for the wording and structure of his pericope of the prophecy of Peter's denial drew on the third gospel—at a point where Luke is independent of Mark. In addition John makes use of one element of this Lucan passage (that of Jesus' intercessory prayer) elsewhere in his last supper account. Finally, the extensive correspondence between the Lucan passage and Jn. 21. 25-18 is demonstrable, whereby it devolves that Lk. 21. 31 f. is a variant of the Jn. 21. 15-18 tradition, belonging like it in a post-resurrection context.

---

in view of his coming death (v. 37), and in order to prepare the disciples for the future, to tell them that, whereas during his lifetime their preaching was welcomed by their hearers, from now on they will have to gird themselves to meet the hostility which will be their lot. That is to say, the future will be harder than the past has been. In John, on the other hand, where Jesus likewise prepares the disciples for the future, above all for his coming death (his "going," or "leaving" them: 13. 33, 36; 14. 25, 28; 16. 27), the time thereafter for the disciples is pictured as not harder, worse, than that when Jesus was with them, but better. They will do greater works than Jesus himself has done (14. 12); their prayers in his name will be answered (16. 12); finally, the Paraclete will impart to them fuller knowledge than they have previously had (16. 12 f.). (It is true that there's a negative side to the future of the disciples and the Church as outlined in John's discourse, i. e. 15. 18, 20, 16. 1, 17. 4, which isn't to be confused with the temporary grief of the disciples which will turn to joy: 16. 20. Also, there's a positive description of the disciples' future in Luke's discourse, in vv. 29 f. But in John the negative is completely subordinate to the positive; and in Luke, vv. 29 f. refers not to the historical future, the time of the Church, but to the end of history.) We see from this how John has transformed the Lucan scene, in accordance with his own view of things (wherein the disciples' grief at Jesus' impending death plays a great rôle), to produce a completely different picture than Luke's, where the disciples' reaction (v. 38) is not one of grief (implying resignation) but rather issues in an attempt to prevent Jesus' death.

CHAPTER EIGHT

FROM THE LAST SUPPER TO THE ARREST

Luke 22. 39-53a / John 18. 1-12

In their accounts of Jesus' actions from the end of the last supper up to and including his arrest, the third and fourth gospels have the following points in common: (a) the disciples are explicitly mentioned as accompanying Jesus as he leaves the meal (Lk. 22. 39b, Jn. 18. 1); (b) Jesus' goal is not called Gethsemane; (c) the place where Jesus was arrested is mentioned as one frquented by him (Lk. 22. 39a, Jn. 18. 12); (d) Jesus is arrested at the conclusion of the scene in which his assailants come upon him (Lk. 22. 54, Jn. 18. 12; συλλαμβάνειν appears in both places); the disciples' use of force therefore represents an effort to prevent his arrest, not to free him, as in Matthew and Mark;[1] (e) the rôle of Judas' kiss is reduced as over against Matthew and Mark;[2] (f) the *right* ear of the highpriest's slave is cut off;[3] (g) the disciples do not flee.[4]

---

[1] Zurhellen, *op. cit.*, p. 40, maintains that Luke and John do not here agree, i. e. that Lk. 22. 54 presupposes the arrest as already having occurred, showing that Luke merely omitted to mention the arrest in v. 48. But ἐσόμενον in v. 49 (D's reading of γενόμενον is clearly secondary) reveals the incorrectness of this view.

[2] John omits it entirely. Luke mentions it in 22. 48—but unlike Matthew and Mark doesn't mention the agreement between Judas and his companions as to what it was to signify. (That this latter really is necessary is shown by the fact that D sy^{p} felt called upon to supply it in Luke's text.) As for 22. 48, it is a question whether it represents Jesus' response to the kiss as it is being delivered (so Zurhellen, *op. cit.*, p. 49, and Bernard and Klostermann in their commentaries, *ad loc.*) or whether with these words Jesus warns Judas to desist from the particular wickedness of a betrayal by means of a kiss, i. e. he prevents the kiss therewith (so Dibelius, *op. cit.*, p. 202 and—following Moffatt—Manson, *op. cit.*, *ad loc.*). The fact that the kiss is not actually mentioned as occurring favors the latter interpretation, in which case Luke agrees with John that the kiss did not occur.

[3] Grant, *op. cit.*, p. 297, cites the fact that τὸ δεξίον in both Lk. 22. 50 and Jn. 18. 10a comes at the end of a sentence, and concludes from this that probably in both cases it constitutes a late addition to the text. But there is no manuscript evidence to support this view; and, if τὸ δεξίον did not originally form part of at least one of the two accounts, how is its existence in either gospel to be explained?

[4] One minor agreement may further be mentioned: τόπος occurs in Lk. 22. 40 and Jn. 18. 2. In addition, there is a similarity of construction between

The first two of these elements are, in Luke, separated from the scene of the arrest by the incident of Jesus' praying and the disciples' sleeping, but it will be convenient to deal with them in connection with the elements centering about Jesus' arrest.

Before trying to evaluate the significance of these agreements, it is important to realize the differences that exist between the Lucan and Johannine accounts of the arrest. In Luke Jesus speaks to Judas concerning the kiss, the disciples ask Jesus if they may use force to defend him, the ear wound is healed by him, and in several sentences (vv. 52 f.) he points out the injustice of what his assailants are doing. John brings none of this, instead he recounts, as Luke does not, that Judas comes accompanied by Roman soldiers and their commander, that Jesus twice asks them whom they seek and upon their answering says twice that he is the man, that they thereupon fall to the ground, that Jesus intercedes on behalf of his disciples, and that Peter and Malchus are the names of the two involved in the ear incident. In view of these divergences, the agreements between the two gospels appear to be isolated ones, occurring in the midst of basically different contexts. We shall see whether further examination confirms this impression. Such an examination will have two goals: first, to determine whether the evidence points to Luke's and John's having drawn on a common source or on two similar sources here, or to John's having drawn on Luke; second, to determine the historical value of the material on which the two accounts agree.

As far as Luke is concerned, there are two possibilities: either he derived these elements from a non-Maran source, or they are the product of his own pen. In connection with two of them, the answer is clear. The notice in Lk. 22. 39 that Jesus went to the Mount of Olives as was his custom derives from, as it agrees with, that in 21. 37 f. (according to which Jesus while in Jerusalem spent his days in the temple teaching and his nights in the Mount of Olives), which clearly stems from Luke's pen [1] and represents his

---

Lk. 22. 49: ἰδόντες δὲ οἱ περὶ αὐτὸν τὸ ἐσόμενον . . . ., and Jn. 18. 4: Ἰησοῦς οὖν εἰδὼς πάντα τὰ ἐρχόμενα ἐπ' αὐτόν . . . .

[1] Mark associates Jesus both with the Mount of Olives (11, 1, 13. 13, 14. 26) and Bethany (11. 1, 11. 11 f., 14. 3) during his period of activity in Jerusalem; Luke's preference for the former has to do with the association in the Marcan tradition of Bethany with the anointing of Jesus, which incident Luke (see above) brings according to another tradition which has nothing to do with that village.

effort to give coherence to the account of Jesus' stay in Jerusalem. [1] Likewise, the notice that it was the chiefpriest's right ear which was cut off stems from the evangelist, as a comparison of Lk. 6. 6 with Mk. 3. 1 makes clear. As for the other points on which Luke agrees with John, the question as to whether or not they originated with the evangelist depends for its answer on whether Luke's only source here was Mark, which he emended extensively, or Mark and another source, from which he derived the rest of what he has in common with John. [2] Taylor [3] cites two elements in Luke which he maintains point to his use of a non-Marcan source here: [4] (a) the reference to Judas as ὁ λεγόμενος 'Ιούδας εἷς τῶν δώδεκα in v. 47, which he sees as explicable only if it comes from a source from which Luke, forgetting that it was unnecessarily elaborate in view of the reference to Judas in 22. 3, took it over; (b) the healing of the ear in Lk. 22. 51 b, which Taylor, [5] finding it incompatible with the ear's having been severed, sees as coming from proto-Luke (in which account he postulates the ear was merely bruised), the detail that the ear was severed being taken over by Luke from Mark. But the reference to Judas, which, as Klostermann has pointed out, [6] is difficult not as regards the ὁ λεγόμενος but as regards the 'Ιούδας, [7] is to be explained as far as the difficult word is concerned precisely on the ground that Luke is following Mark at this point despite the 22. 3 reference; this, coupled with the occurrence of ὄχλος and εἷς τῶν δώδεκα in both Mk. 14. 43 and 22. 47, proves that v. 47 does not derive from a non-Marcan source. As for Taylor's objection to the healing of a severed ear, it is based on a rationa-

---

[1] The effect, in conjunction with Luke's dissolution of Mark's scheme of division of Jesus' Jerusalem period into days, is also to give the impression of a longer period of activity of Jesus in Jerusalem, comparable to that in Galilee and on the journey, as Conzelmann has recently pointed out (*op. cit.*, pp. 63 f.).

[2] That Luke used Mark here is clear from 22. 52 f., also from ἔτι αὐτοῦ λαλοῦντος in v. 47 and perhaps εἷς τις in v. 50.

[3] Taylor, *op. cit.*, p. 45 ff.

[4] To this source, his proto-Luke, he attributes the entire passage (except for v. 52 f. and the mention of the ear as being severed in v. 50), including the note on the right ear and the placing of the arrest at the scene's end.

[5] Following E. R. Micklem, *Miracles and the New Psychology*, pp. 127 ff.

[6] Klostermann, *op. cit.*, *ad loc.*

[7] One would expect, after 22. 3, and in view of the fact that Luke knows of two different disciples named Judas (6. 16), the phrase ὁ λεγόμενος 'Ισκαριώτης.

listic view of Jesus' healing power which the evangelist did not share.

The evidence, then, does not support the contention that Luke for 22. 47-53 had a second source. [1] Moreover, a perfectly satisfactory explanation exists of Luke's departures from Mark at this point, one not involving the postulation of a second source. This is that Luke has rewritten Mark here in order to produce a scene dominated by Jesus. [2] Whereas in Mark's account, except for the statement he makes after his arrest, Jesus is passive, and the scene is dominated by Judas and his kiss, by the arrest, by the cutting off of the ear, and by the flight of the disciples and the youth, Luke produces a scene in which Jesus speaks to Judas, [3] answers the disciples' question, heals the ear, and points out (as in Mark) the needlessness of an arrest under such circumstances. In line with this is the fact that Luke has him arrested only at the end of the scene: till then he is, literally, free to dominate the situation. [4] As for the fact that the disciples do not abandon Jesus, Luke's tendency to spare the disciples wherever possible

---

[1] Schniewind, *op. cit.*, pp. 35 f. (following Johannes Weiss), on the basis of the presence of the chiefpriests, temple guards and elders in v. 52 and of the similarity which he finds between Jesus' words in vv. 52 b-53 and those in Jn. 18. 20, regards vv. 52 f. as the unclear reflection of a tradition of Jesus' examination before the highpriest, a tradition clearly reflected in Jn. 18. 20. In such a scene, he feels, the Jewish notables would of course have been present, as they would not at the arrest, and there Jesus' words would fit better than in the commotion of an arrest scene. He therefore sees here the influence of a Johannine tradition on Luke. But in fact the dignitaries have been added by Luke in order to provide a more important audience for Jesus' words in vv. 52 b-53, one which the evangelist felt was required by the sense of these words. Vv. 52 f. are substantially derived from Mark, where the chiefpriests and elders play no part—for which verses there is then no good reason (for Jesus' words in Mark and Luke are not *that* similar to those in Jn. 18. 20, nor do they fit so badly into an arrest scene) to assign them to an examination scene.

[2] So Creed, *op. cit.*, *ad loc.*, Grant, *op. cit.*, p. 296, Dibelius, *op. cit.*, pp. 201 f. and Bultmann, *Geschichte der synoptischen Tradition*, p. 303.

[3] Whether or not Luke means to imply that Judas' kiss didn't actually occur, the dominant rôle in connection with it is not played by Judas, as in Mark, but by Jesus with his words directed to Judas.

[4] This view of the origin of this detail is surely sounder than one seeing here an echo of an historical tradition, for it is exceedingly unlikely that Jesus would not immediately be arrested by his assailants. That the detail originated with Luke is confirmed by his use in connection with it of συλλαμβάνειν, which, appearing as it does eleven times in Luke-Acts (in five of which it has the meaning 'sieze' in connection with an arrest), is a favorite word of his.

(cf. for example his omission of Mk. 10. 35-40) is well-known; the omission of the flight, which conflicts not only with Matthew's and Mark's account but with material Luke himself brings (i.e. 22. 32b), clearly originates with the third evangelist. We conclude, then, that Luke has not derived his points of contact with John from a non-Marcan source—and therewith the question as to the historical value of the Luke—John contacts at this point, as far as Luke is concerned, is also answered.

John shares with Luke in connection with the arrest not only the points listed above, but also an interest in producing a scene dominated by Jesus—indeed, he has been even freer than Luke in this regard, producing a scene where Jesus is not merely dominant, he is sovereign. The Judas kiss is completely eliminated: Jesus does not wait to be identified by any one; instead he goes out to meet Judas and those accompanying him, completely dominates an exchange with them in the course of which (struck down by Jesus' supernatural power?) [1] they fall to the ground; he then concerns himself to protect his disciples, and concludes the scene by rejecting the disciples' attempt at resistance with a statement of his submission to his Father's will. Only after the scene, properly speaking, is over, is he arrested—as was true in Luke. [2] This presents a picture of Jesus in accord with that found throughout the fourth gospel, [3] but the evidence here points not to John's having independently constructed the scene but to his having found in Luke's gospel an account of the arrest partially satisfactory to him (as Mark's was not), [4] which he therefore utilized in the course of composing his scene. [5] So he took over from

---

[1] So Bauer, *Das Johannesevangelium, ad loc.*

[2] John records that Jesus was bound upon arrest; Luke does not mention that Jesus ever was bound, whereas in Mark and Matthew's accounts he is bound not at the time of his arrest but when he is led by the Jews to Pilate. On this detail in John see E. Bickermann, "Utilitas Crucis," *Revue de l'Histoire des Religions*, 1935, p. 221.

[3] e.g. 13. 31, where Jesus can say, before the crucifixion and resurrection, that he is glorified.

[4] That John found Mark's account unacceptable is indicated by the fact that he took over almost nothing from it; he may be following Mark in his use of παίειν and ὠτάριον in 18. 10, but he does not follow him (as Luke does) at the one point in the Marcan account where Jesus plays an active rôle, i. e. in his statement to his captors after his arrest.

[5] Bultmann, *Das Evangelium des Johannes, ad loc.*, postulates as the evangelist's only source for 18. 1-11 a non-synoptic, written one, from which he derived vv. 4 f. and 10 f., and therefore the detail as to which

Luke the timing of the arrest,[1] and, following up Luke's partial measure, completely eliminated the Judas kiss; he also followed Luke in deleting mention of the flight of the disciples.[2] Further, he derived from Luke such details as the fact that it was the slave's right ear which was cut off,[3] and that Jesus had often before been in the place where he was arrested. That the latter came to John from Luke, despite the fact that in Luke it is the Mount of Olives which Jesus is mentioned as frequenting, in John a garden,[4] is made likely by the fact that in John, though the

ear it was, as well as the picture of a soverign Jesus insofar as this was already implied in Jesus' asking those coming upon him who it was they sought. He defends this postulation as regards v. 4 f. on the ground that otherwise the mention of Jesus in v. 5, after the mention of him in v. 3, is inexplicable. But Bertram's explanation (*Die Leidensgeschichte Jesu und der Christuskult*, pp. 52 f.) of this feature of v. 5 is preferable; he sees in v. 5 a correction of previous tradition, a correction according to which Jesus had to reveal himself to his attackers despite the fact that one of the attackers present, Judas, could have done so. As for vv. 19 f., Bultmann attributes them to a source on the ground that the names Peter and Malchus represent a legendary addition to the ear incident which isn't to be attributed to the evangelist. Whether or not he is right as regards the two names, there is no reason to ascribe the two verses in their entirety, including the right ear detail, to a source— it is more natural to see this detail as derived by the evangelist from Luke (so Barrett, *op. cit.*, *ad loc.*), whose rôle as a source for John in 18. 1-11 Bultmann completely fails to perceive. This is not to say that John had no source of information at this point other than Mark and Luke (to see him in 18. 11 as directly dependent on Matt. 26. 52 is, despite the striking parallel, unjustified, because the two sentences have no words in common beyond μαχαίρα), or that he invented such details as Peter, Malchus and the presence at the arrest of the Roman σπεῖρα (on which last see Goguel, *The Life of Jesus*, pp. 374, 417, and following him Cullmann, *op. cit.*, p. 45). However, that he had any *written* non-synoptic source here is exceedingly unlikely; the scene as we have it is substantially the result of his composition using Luke as his point of departure and employing in addition elements of oral tradition.

[1] This is confirmed by his use in this connection of συλλαμβάνειν, a word which never otherwise appears in his gospel and which he here took over from Luke (for whose use of it see p. 50, nt. 4).

[2] John's position here is not fully clear. In 16. 32 he brings a word of Jesus which presupposes the flight of the disciples, which he includes despite his failure to report the flight. Was he unsure whether or not the flight occurred? In view of the many passages in his passion and resurrection account which presuppose that the disciples did not all flee, i.e. 18. 15, 19. 26, 19. 35, 20. 3, we must assume that John's position on the matter was clear, and that 16. 32 was either an oversight or is of secondary importance.

[3] Schniewind, *op. cit.*, p. 35, sees in the occurrence of the right ear detail in Luke and John only a phenomenon of common tradition, but that is to fail to interpret the evidence in the most natural way.

[4] From the mention of the Kedron brook in John it is clear that John does not point to a different location for the arrest than that in the synoptics.

garden plays an important rôle, it does so only afterwards, i.e. in connection with the crucifixion, burial and resurrection (19. 41, 20. 13). [1] Further, the construction in Jn. 18. 4 cited above [2] may have been suggested to John by a reading of Lk. 22. 49; τόπος, however, is too common a word in the fourth gospel (it occurs seventeen times there) for its occurrence in Lk. 22. 40 to be signifiant as far as its use in Jn. 18. 2 is concerned.

We've already mentioned that neither Luke nor John mention Gethsemane; as a negative agreement, it is not significant, having in Luke to do with his dislike of Semitic place names (cf. his omission of Golgotha in 23. 33), in John with the fact that Gethsemane was associated in the tradition with Jesus' praying in a manner John felt was unworthy of him. That John, like Luke, explicitly mentions the disciples in recounting that Jesus left the last supper cannot be cited with certainty as indicating further dependence of John on Luke, though such is possible. This mention, lacking in Mark and Matthew, is not necessitated by the fact that due to the intrusion of the last discourses in John the disciples have not been mentioned since the thirteenth chapter and that therefore without an explicit reference to them it would not be clear who was meant, [3] for even in John it would be clear who was meant if it was merely stated, as in Mark (14. 26) and Matthew (26. 30), that "they" left the meal; rather, whereas Matthew and Mark lump Jesus and the disciples together here, Luke and John, putting characteristically more weight on the central figure, say that Jesus left, adding that the disciples accompanied him. The occurrence of this minor emendation in both Luke and John may, therefore, be due not to John's following Luke, but to the two of them sharing the same interest, that of emphasizing Jesus' role, at this point. [4]

Hoskyns, *Journal of Theological Studies*, 1920, pp. 214 f., sees the garden, which here and later in the passion plays an important role, as analogous for the evangelist to the Garden of Eden.

[1] Although Jesus' having often been in the garden is mentioned not for its own sake, but in order to explain Judas' knowledge, it may be that John means to imply that Jesus was not seeking to avoid arrest (cf. 13. 27, and the absence of Jesus' anxious prayer before his arrest).

[2] P. 47, nt. 4.

[3] So Schniewind, *op. cit.*, p. 33.

[4] Two further, minor parallels between Lucan and Johannine tradition may here be mentioned. In Acts 1. 16 Judas is referred to as the guide of those arresting Jesus, which corresponds to the notice in Jn. 18. 2 that Judas knew where Jesus was. The emphasis in the Lucan-Johannine tradition, therefore, is on Judas as showing the assailants *where* Jesus was, whereas

John's dependence on Luke here must not, indeed, be understood as a passive one, as the differences between Luke and John make clear. John used Luke because Luke recorded a scene acceptable to him as Mark's was not, a scene, indeed, which suggested to him what the scene he would record in his gospel should be like. But where Luke departed from what John felt was the correct presentation he did not hesitate not to follow him. So he deleted the incident of Jesus' praying (and the disciples' sleeping which is connected with it) which occurs at the beginning of the scene in Luke as well as in Mark and Matthew. He was not content with this; Jesus' concluding statement in John's account (in 18. 11b) is, in its use of ποτήριον (it is the only occurrence of the word in the fourth gospel), clearly a comment on the impossibility of the prayer (where ποτήριον also appears) which Luke and the other evangelists record at this point. John was more consistent here than Luke, [1] but he nevertheless followed Luke, strengthening the emphasis he found in him. However, due to this shared emphasis, it is not correct to see, as appeared at first to be the case, the agreements between Luke and John merely as isolated ones within differing contexts. Indeed, not the details but the emphasis on the dominant position of Christ is the important thing the two have in common.

We have therewith found the answers to the two questions we asked above. For the positive similarities between Luke and John, with the possible exception of the mention of the disciples at the conclusion of the last supper, John is dependent on Luke; and what they have in common does not derive from a (possibly historically accurate) source of Luke's but from his own conception of what must have occurred at the time of the arrest.

Matthew and Mark, emphasizing the kiss, underline that Jesus showed them *who* Jesus was. Finally, there is a similarity between the metaphor employed in Luke and John in connection with Judas and his company. In Luke (22. 53), Jesus says as he is arrested, "This is your hour and the power of darkness;" Jn. 13. 30 states, in the course of the last supper account, "Taking the morsel (Judas) went out immediately; it was night." That the literal sense does not exhaust the meaning of this last, so that a parallel to Lk. 22. 53 is here to be found, is clear from Jn. 9. 4.

[1] To follow the Marcan tradition of the prayer would for John be inconsistent not only with the general picture of Jesus he transmits, but specifically with 13. 27 b; Luke, on the other hand, follows Mark despite the tradition which, in 12. 50, he independently offers. Indeed, if 22. 43 f. belong to the original Lucan text, Luke actually increases the tension between this scene and the 12. 50 statement.

CHAPTER NINE

JESUS' APPEARANCE BEFORE THE JEWISH AUTHORITIES AND PETER'S DENIAL

Luke 22. 53b-71 / John 18. 13-28

Luke's and John's accounts of Jesus' appearance before the Jewish authorities agree in that neither constitutes a formal trial with witnesses called and a verdict handed down, whereas in Mark and Matthew this is the case. Further, as we'll see, there are signs that Luke agrees with John in seeing Annas as the primary Jewish dignitary present at the hearing. [1]

[1] Though in Luke and John, as in the other two gospels, the account of the hearing is closely connected with Peter's denial, there is only one slight parallel between Luke's and John's accounts of the latter. In Luke, Peter's second denial takes the form ἄνθρωπε, οὐκ εἰμί, and it is possible that this has influenced John in his phrasing of the first and second denials (both: οὐκ εἰμί); if so, his reason for following Luke here but not elsewhere in the passage is that Luke provided him with a phrase contrasting nicely with Jesus' twice-repeatedly ἐγω εἰμί in John's arrest scene. However, it is also possible that the agreement here is purely accidental; the answer in Peter's mouth οὐκ εἰμί is a most natural one, and John, in the course of producing an account of the denial more stylized than those in the synoptic gospels (see for example the fact that the statements accusing Peter all take the form of questions addressed to him), may have hit upon it quite independently. Schniewind, *op. cit.*, pp. 49 ff. (following H. J. Holtzmann, *op. cit.*, p. 77) maintains that Luke and John for their accounts of the denial draw on related traditions. According to him, John, in whose account the denial is interrupted by the hearing, after which Jesus is led away to Caiaphas' palace, recounts directly what in Luke is less clearly narrated, or rather hinted at; Schniewind believes, that is to say, that the hour intermission mentioned in 22. 57 and Jesus' glance at Peter mentioned in 22. 61 presuppose that Jesus was led out of the palace and passed by Peter in doing so. The correspondence, however, which Schniewind maintains exists between the two accounts, does not stand the text of a close analysis of the texts. The hour mentioned in Luke occurs after the second denial, whereas the hearing in John occurs after the first; and διαστάσης ὡσεὶ ὥρας μιᾶς in v. 59 is Luke's creation which he brings instead of Mark's μετὰ μικρόν because, after the μετὰ βραχύ in v. 58 with which Luke replaces Mk. 14. 68 b, μετὰ μικρόν would constitute no buildup, which is what Luke, who is leading up to the climax of the third denial capped by the crowing cock and Jesus' glance, wants. Further, it is clear that Jesus' gaze in Luke is created by the evangelist in order to enhance the climax; it comes, moreover, after the third denial, whereas in John's account Jesus is led out of the palace after the first. Actually both Luke and John derive the rudiments of their denial accounts from Mark. For Mark this

However, the divergencies between Luke and John here, which we shall have to take into account in analyzing the similarities, are marked. Luke records that Jesus (followed by Peter) is led to the palace of the highpriest, [1] whereupon Peter's denial is recorded in its entirety; then Jesus is mocked by his captors, led next morning before the Sanhedrin (called in v. 66 the πρεσβυτέριον), examined and sent to Pilate. In John Jesus is taken to Annas, whereupon Peter (gaining admission to the palace by means of "another disciple") denies Jesus once; Jesus is then questioned by Caiaphas, [2] struck by one of his underlings and sent by Annas to Caiaphas who sends him on to Pilate — and Peter, remaining behind at Annas', denies Jesus a second and third time. All this occurs at night in John's account.

To understand the significance of the common Lucan-Johannine elements here, we must ascertain what the sources of both were at this point. Luke uses Mark in his account of the examination scene, [3] but departs from him as far as the order of the events is concerned as well as in the elements which he has in common with John. [4] John's account as it stands is impossible. Why is Jesus taken to Annas' palace if he is to be questioned by Caiaphas there, and why, if Caiaphas questioned him at Annas', does Annas then send him to Caiaphas? Why is Jesus' transferal to Caiaphas' mentioned when absolutely nothing of what went on there is described? Further, how is the "other disciple" able to introduce Peter into Annas' palace on the basis of his acquaintance with Caiaphas (for so v. 16 must be understood), and why does Peter, when Jesus is led to Caiaphas, remain behind at Annas' palace? [5]

---

is clear from παιδίσκη in 22. 56 (cf. Mk. 14. 66), from 22. 57 (cf. Mk. 14. 68), from ἐπ' ἀληθείας and γὰρ Γαλιλαῖος in 22. 56 (cf. Mk. 14. 70), and from 22. 61 b (cf. Mk. 14. 72 b). For John see nt. 11 below.

[1] On who is meant, see below.

[2] His identity as the highpriest referred to in vv. 16, 19 and 22, *as the text stands*, is assured by vv. 13 and 24.

[3] Compare 22. 67a, 69, 71 and Mk 14. 61 b, 62, 63 b. He probably also uses Mark for the mocking: see προφήτευσον in Mk. 14. 65 and Lk. 22. 64.

[4] How cleverly Luke alters Mark is indicated by his use of Mark in v. 71 which, because of his omission of Mk. 14. 55-60, no longer means, as in Mark, "Why do we need further witnesses?", but "Why do we need any witnesses at all?"

[5] Following Euthymius Zigabenus, Zahn and Plummer in their commentaries, *ad loc.*, postulate that Annas and Caiaphas lived in different parts of the same palace, but there is no justification in the text whatever for this assumption. Since such a state of affairs is not what one would expect, it

A number of critics [1] see the difficulties here as the result of John's having set out to combine all the synoptic traditions, producing two hearings to correspond with Mk. 14. 53-64 and 15. 1, and drawing Caiaphas' name from the Marcan-Matthean tradition and Annas' from the Lucan tradition. But, though as we shall see the third evangelist thought Annas examined Jesus, nevertheless this is not clear from Lk. 22. 54, and John's interest in Luke was hardly so extensive that he would have drawn conclusions for Lk. 22. 54 from Lk. 3. 2 and Acts 4. 6. Further, it is inconceivable that John could have set out from scratch, as it were, to compose a passage on the basis of synoptic sources and have produced an account as problematical as this. [2]

A better explanation is that John composed the core of vv. 12-27, consisting of vv. 12-13a, 15-23, and 25b-27, at an early stage in the composition of his gospel, and added 13b, 14 and 24-25a to it later, at which time the difficulties arose. John composed the core on the basis of two sources, one Mark, and the other a source in which Annas examined Jesus and in which he was called the highpriest. John adopted this terminology in the core passage (see vv. 15, 19, 22); either he thought Annas was the highpriest at the time of Jesus' death (in which case 11. 49-51 represents an addition to the gospel made by John at the time when he added 18. 13b, 14, 24-25a, which, considering the striking similarity between 18. 14 and 11. 49 ff., is quite likely), or, if 11. 49-51 was a part of the gospel from the beginning, and John knew that Caiaphas was highpriest, [3] he understood ἀρχιερεύς for Annas in the loose sense, i.e. as designating an ex-highpriest. [4] From Mark he derived the rudiments of the denial scene as he recounted it in the core passage, [5] and for the examination scene he utilized Marcan

---

would have been expressly mentioned had it been true (so correctly Bultmann, *op. cit.*, *ad loc.*). Further, the change of order brought by sy[s] clearly represents, as the commentators acknowledge, a secondary effort to eradicate the difficulties.

[1] i.e. Klostermann, Hoskyns and Barrett in their commentaries, *ad loc.*

[2] John as we've seen did combine the Marcan and Lucan anointing accounts, with resultant uneveness in the Johannine text—but the uneveness there is not to be compared with what we find here.

[3] In either case the extremely problematical phrase τοῦ ἐνιαυτοῦ ἐκείνου in 11. 49 b and 18. 19, on which see Bultmann, *op. cit.*, *ad loc.*, does not speak well for John's knowledge of the highpriestly office.

[4] This meaning for the title "highpriest" is attested by Jeremias, *Jerusalem zur Zeit Jesu*, II B, p. 58.

[5] This is indicated, as Bultmann and Barrett in their commentaries

elements [1] (and conceivably a scene from Acts), [2] which he recast [3] in constructing a scene whose brevity and unclarity [4] indicate that he took little interest in it. [5] (Whether or not he derived the picture of the hearing as stripped of all formal character, i.e. without witnesses and a sentence, from his non-Marcan source is a question with which we shall deal below.) To the core passage John later added 13b (from πρῶτον on), 14 and 24-25a. The purpose

---

agree, by the fact that the gatekeeper in John's account is a girl (παιδίσκη), a detail which, in its improbability (the scene occurs at night!) came about as the result of John's having drawn on Mark insofar as there also the first person to suspect Peter is a girl (though, since she is not a gatekeeper, no problem exists in regard to her in Mark). John did not derive the gatekeeper notice from another source, but introduced it in connection with the introduction of the gate motif and of the "other disciple" (both of which are his own creation, as Bultmann, *op. cit., ad loc.*, has seen). Further, the fact that the denial follows immediately upon Peter's entry into the highpriest's palace, without the hearing intervening between the two, is likewise to be explained not on the basis of another source, but on the basis of John's introduction of the "other disciple" into the account; he reasoned that the gatekeeper's attention would immediately be drawn to Peter by the other disciple's negotiations with her on Peter's behalf.

[1] V. 20 is a reflection of Mk. 14. 49, as Hoskyns, Klostermann and Bultmann have seen. Further, the blow in 22 quite likely derives from Mk. 14. 65: ῥαπίσμα is used in both cases. Also, Jesus' statement in v. 21, "Why ask me? Ask those who heard what I spoke to them," contains an oblique reference to the witnesses of Mk. 14. 56-61; the effect of this statement, as Barrett, *op. cit., ad loc.*, points out, is to exclude the taking of testimony recorded in Mark.

[2] The similarity of Jn. 18. 19 ff. to Acts 23. 1 ff. is evident when one realizes that in the latter Paul is struck by a Jew, and that the issue of his disrespect towards the highpriest is raised. But the details (e.g. the highpriest's behavior, Paul's response to the blow, the fact that in Acts Paul's words which are called disrespectful constitute his response to the blow, whereas in John Jesus' words which are called disrespectful cause the blow) and the vocabulary are so different that it is very unlikely that John, except perhaps unconsciously, was here utilizing Acts. We can, at all events, not postulate on the basis of this one parallel that John knew Acts.

[3] The expressions used are Johannine. παρρησίᾳ occurs nine times in John, once in Mark, never in Matthew; Luke uses μετὰ παρρησίας. ἐν συναγωγῇ and ἐν κρυπτῷ occur only in John—elsewhere in the New Testament one finds ἐν τῇ συναγωγῇ and ἐν τῷ κρυπτῷ. For the use of ὁ κόσμος to mean "everybody" cf. Jn. 12. 19.

[4] It isn't clear, for instance, why the hearing is broken off. Is it terminated as a result of the brutality of the underling who strikes Jesus (so Klostermann, *op. cit., ad loc.*), or because Jesus' statement in 23 is unanswerable (so Hoskyns, *The Fourth Gospel, ad loc.*)? At any rate, John's point is to show the Jews' complete lack of interest in observing any legal proprieties.

[5] This lack of interest is due to the fact that in John's gospel Jesus has already earlier publicly proclaimed his position (e.g. 5. 17 f., 5. 26, 7. 46, 8. 58 f.), whereas in the synoptics this first occurs in the Jewish examination.

of this alteration was to make his account conform to the view that Caiaphas had examined Jesus. [1] John now meant ἀρχιερεύς in 19 to refer to Caiaphas. The confusion in his account arose from the fact that he did not wish to suppress the Annas tradition, which was the original one he advocated, entirely, though he did in fact reduce Annas' rôle to the point where his only action was to send Jesus to Caiaphas' palace. [2]

The Johannine source in which Annas is called highpriest has a counterpart in Luke, in whose gospel Caiaphas is never called highpriest, but where Annas twice is (Lk. 3. 2, Acts 4. 6), [3] which means that in all likelihood Luke understood ἀρχιερεύς in Mk. 14.53, and therefore in Lk. 22. 54, as referring to Annas. [4] Was he confirmed in this view by a knowledge of the non-Marcan account of the examination which John employed? Before we can answer this, we must discuss Luke's and John's other agreement here, their agreement on the fact that Jesus' examination by the Jews didn't constitute a formal trial. In regard to this latter we must determine whether Luke and John omitted the hearing of witnesses and the sentencing contained in Mark's account on the basis of their own theological interests, [5] or on the basis of non-Marcan

[1] This view is expressly held by Matthew alone among the other evangelists (26. 27). Even in the unlikely event that John knew Matthew's gospel, he shows himself so little influenced by it elsewhere that we cannot on that basis alone account for his behavior here. Since Caiaphas was highpriest at the time of Jesus' death, Mk. 14. 53, 61 and 63 on the most natural reading support Matthew's assertion; nevertheless, as we'll see, it's quite possible that the most obvious reading of Mark isn't the correct one. At any event, we must assume that others besides Matthew believed that Caiaphas had examined Jesus—otherwise John would not have acted here as he did.

[2] Wellhausen and Bultmann in their commentaries, *ad loc.*, Zurhellen, *op. cit.*, p. 50 and Goguel, *op. cit.*, p. 79, concur in the view that the Caiaphas element is a later addition to the original Johannine Annas tradition.

[3] Bultmann, *op. cit.*, p. 497, nt. 4 (following Wellhausen and G. Hölscher) maintains that "and Caiaphas" is a later addition to the texts of Lk. 3. 2 and Acts. 4. 6, but there is no evidence to support this. Moreover, the two texts are not to be explained on the ground that Luke is here using ἀρχιερέυς loosely to refer to an ex-highpriest; such a use is hardly possible in a sentence in which immediately thereafter the incumbent highpriest is named—and without title! No, Luke clearly thought Annas was the incumbent highpriest.

[4] This is all the more likely since Mark, whom Luke knew, never states who the highpriest was—whereas Matthew, whom Luke did not know, does so. Luke may not have been absolutely sure who did examine Jesus, which would account for his reduction of the role of the highpriest, who in his account is not mentioned as personally examining Jesus.

[5] This view is maintained for Luke by Bultmann, *Geschichte der synop-*

sources (perhaps, for John, Luke's account). Several factors speak in favor of the second view for both evangelists. As far as Luke is concerned, in view of what we know about his theology, no good theological motivation for his recasting of the trial scene can be discerned; secondly, as his corresponding alteration of Mk. 10. 33 in Lk. 18. 31 shows, his alteration of the trial scene was no casual, much less an accidental, [1] one. Together, these factors indicate that he was here following a second source. As for John, there is a passage in his gospel, i.e. 10. 22-39, which points to his having derived the picture of a hearing without witnesses or sentence neither from his own imagination nor from Luke, but from the same non-Johannine source from which Luke derived it. In 10. 22-29 he brings an account of a questioning of Jesus by the Jews which is strikingly close to the non-Marcan material Luke brings in 22. 67-71. In both accounts Jesus' claim to be messiah is dealt with separately from his claim to be the son of God (Lk. 22. 67, 70 cf. Jn. 10. 24 f., 29 ff.), whereas in Mark (14. 61) they are combined. In both accounts the Jews take action against Jesus not on the basis of the first but the second assertion (Jn. 10. 31, 36 cf. Lk. 22. 71). Above all, there is a striking verbal similarity between the two as regards the question and answer in Lk. 22. 67 and in Jn. 10. 24b-25a. On the other hand, one significant difference exists between the two accounts, and that is that whereas Jesus answers equivocally in Luke (in 22. 67b-68a and 70b) [2] he does not do so in John (10. 25, 29 ff.). Both the similarities and the differences are explicable on the supposition that John knew the account of the Jewish hearing which Luke combined with Mark, [3] and that he used it as the basis of the ch. 10 scene occurring earlier in his gospel, changing Jesus' answer into a direct one in conformity with his picture of Jesus as openly proclaiming his messianic position

tischen Tradition, supplement to p. 303, who here follows Finegan, *Die Ueberlieferung der Leidens- und Auferstehungsgeschichte*, pp. 23 ff. It is maintained for John by Klostermann, Hoskyns and Barrett in their commentaries, *ad loc.*, and Finegan, *op. cit.*, p. 45.

[1] This must be stressed in refuting the position of Finegan, *op. cit.*, p. 25, who holds that Luke meant in 22. 71 what Mark states in 14. 64 b, but merely did not say so expressly.

[2] On this see Cullmann, *The Christology of the New Testament*, p. 120.

[3] That John knew and drew in chs. 10 and 19 on Luke's non-Marcan source rather than Luke himself follows from the fact that only the non-Marcan elements of the examination scene are used by him in 10. 22-39. This points to his having known them in a form where they were not, as in Lk. 22. 66-71, already mixed with Marcan elements.

during his lifetime. If John used this written source (for that it was written is clear from the verbal similarity between Lk. 22. 67 and Jn. 10. 24b-25a) in ch. 10 there is every reason to think that he also used it in constructing the corresponding passage in his gospel (19. 18-23), and that, as Luke did, he derived from it the picture of an informal hearing, without witnesses and sentence. Since, as we saw, John also derived the information that Annas examined Jesus from a source, and since it is unlikely that he here possessed two different non-Marcan sources, we may assume that John derived the Annas information from his and Luke's common source—and that Luke was confirmed by the source in his view that Mk. 14. 53 referred to Annas. [1] Moreover, the vocabulary of this source is closer to that generally used by John than that used by Luke; [2] this points to the likelihood that the source stemmed from an area where the fourth but not the third evangelist was at home.

One question remains to be asked, that of the historical value of the information brought by the source. As for the statement that Annas not Caiaphas examined Jesus, [3] what we know of Annas,

[1] Did Luke derive the order and chronology of the denial, mocking and examination events from this source? The answer is no. Luke's departures from Mark in this regard were due to a desire to simplify Mark's complex account, producing an account entailing only one meeting of the Sanhedrin (and that one, in accordance with the Jewish legal code—see *Sanhedrin* IV 1—not at night) and assigning the mistreatment of Jesus, with greater plausibility, to the attendants at the priest's palace rather than the Sanhedrin members. Confirmation of this is to be found in the fact that Luke in 19. 45 condenses John's two trips into Jerusalem into one in the same way in which he here substitutes one Sanhedrin meeting for two. Furthermore, if Luke's and John's source had contained an account of the denial and mocking, we could expect that John as well as Luke would have drawn on it at these points and that their accounts in this regard would be similar; but this is not the case. There is, in fact, no reason to think that the source contained more than an account of the one examination scene before Annas.

[2] A glance at a concordance shows how much more often πιστεύειν appears in John than in Luke. Likewise, ἐρωτᾶν with the meaning "ask a question" occurs fifteen times in John, but only four times in Luke.

[3] A critical analysis of the four gospels provides no support for the view, advanced by Bernard, *op. cit.*, *ad loc.*, and Schniewind, *op. cit.*, pp. 39 f., that Jesus was examined separately by *both* Caiaphas and Annas. Schniewind, *op. cit.*, pp. 39 f., 52, maintains that at the bottom of both Luke's and John's accounts lies the same, historically authentic scheme of a hearing before Annas followed by a second (the decisive one) before Caiaphas. He sees the contents of the Annas hearing as preserved in John but not in Luke because Luke did not possess a clear record of the events; the result was that within the frame of the (Annas) trial which he brought Luke set the contents of the

whose four sons and son-in-law were later highpriests, and whose deposition by the Roman procurator Valerius Gratus could have no validity to the Jews, [1] makes it likely that he actually did examine Jesus. [2] The fact that Luke thought he and not Caiaphas was highpriest at the time of Jesus' death, though Caiaphas held the office for almost twenty years, shows what a position Annas must have had. Moreover, the evidence for Caiaphas' having examined Jesus is not so great as it at first appears. As already mentioned, Mark never says that the highpriest to whom he in 14. 53 etc. refers is Caiaphas, and in view of the lack of unanimity among the evangelists as to who at the time *was* highpriest, it is illegitimate to cite him, as the commentators without exception do, as supporting Matthew's view rather than Luke's. Indeed it is likely that Annas examined Jesus, and that as an ex-highpriest of great stature he was called by Mark (who never mentions either Annas or Caiaphas by name) simply ὁ ἀρχιερεύς; Mathew, however, did not understand this, but knew that Caiaphas had been then incumbent, and so, adding Caiaphas' name, unwittingly originated the Caiaphas tradition. As far as the lack of a sentence is concerned, the fact that an informal hearing of the Sanhedrin was not against Jewish legal regulations, whereas a formal meeting issuing in an immediate capital conviction was, [3] speaks for its historicity; [4] nevertheless, certainty on this point isn't possible, as it is extremely likely that the Jewish authorities, angry, afraid,

---

Caiaphas hearing. The proof of this Schniewind sees in Lk. 22. 54 and 66, in which, following Holtzmann, *op. cit.*, p. 76, he finds the traces of Luke's original knowledge of two trials. John, on the other hand, he sees as leaving out the hearing before Caiaphas which was originally a part of his tradition, and cites as proof the fact that the sentence handed down in the Caiaphas trial is presupposed in Jn. 18. 31. This hypothesis is far-fetched indeed. Lk. 22. 54 and 22. 66 stem not from a source of Luke's but (see nt. 25) from the evangelist himself; moreover, Luke in no way shares John's scheme of two examinations, which scheme John did not derive from previous tradition but rather (see pp. 84 f. above) unwittingly created.

[1] See Schürer, *Geschichte des Jüdischen Volkes*, 4th ed., II, p. 214, on the politically influential rôle of deposed highpriests.

[2] Cullmann, *The State in the New Testament*, p. 46, supports this view.

[3] According to *Sanhedrin* IV 1.

[4] Cullmann, *op. cit.*, pp. 44 f., following Goguel, regards it as historical. A further point in favor of it is that according to it the Jews took offense not at Jesus' claim to be messiah but to be the son of God, which makes sense in view of what we know about the Jewish attitude toward messianic pretendents as well as what we know about the title son of God as used by Jesus. (On this see Cullmann, *The Christology of the New Testament*, pp. 279 ff.)

and determined to make a speedy end of Jesus, did not bother to observe the letter of the law.[1]

To sum up: we discern that in their accounts of Jesus' examination by the Jews both Luke and John drew, in addition to Mark, on the same written, non-Marcan account of the scene, and that in it Annas examined Jesus and the examination was an informal one; the first of these elements (with which Mark very likely agrees) is probably, the second possibly, historical. And John, in addition, made use of this source in a passage occuring earlier in his gospel.

[1] So Dalman, *Jesus-Jeshua*, p. 99. The issue of whether or not the Jews had the power to carry out capital punishment at the time of Jesus' death isn't germane to our subject; if they did (so Lietzmann, "Der Prozess Jesu," *Sitzungsbericht der preussischen Akademie der Wissenschaften*, 1931, p. 313) then the accounts of all four evangelists of the hearing before the Jews are unhistorical; but see against Lietzmann's position Jeremias, *Zeitschrift für die Neutestamentliche Wissenschaft*, 1950 f., pp. 145-150.

CHAPTER TEN

THE TRIAL BEFORE PILATE

Luke 23. 1-25 / John 18. 29-19. 16

The Lucan and Johannine accounts of Jesus' trial before Pilate have the following points in common: (a) Pilate makes three declarations in Jesus' favor; in Luke he declares once that he finds Jesus absolutely innocent (23. 4: οὐδὲν εὑρίσκω αἴτιον ἐν τῷ ἀνθρώπῳ τούτῳ) and twice that he finds him innocent of any capital crime (23. 15: ἰδοὺ οὐδὲν ἄξιον θανάτου ἐστὶν πεπραγμένον αὐτῷ, 23. 22: οὐδὲν αἴτιον θανάτου εὗρον ἐν αὐτῷ); in John all three declarations of innocence are unqualified: 18. 38 (ἐγὼ οὐδεμίαν εὑρίσκω ἐν αὐτῷ αἰτίαν), 19. 4 (οὐδεμίαν αἰτίαν εὑρίσκω ἐν αὐτῷ), 19. 6 (ἐγὼ γὰρ οὐχ εὑρίσκω ἐν αὐτῷ αἰτίαν); (b) the parallel in conection with the first of these statements goes further, embracing Pilate's preceding question σὺ εἶ ὁ βασιλεὺς τῶν Ἰουδαίων, and Jesus' answer σὺ λέγεις (Lk. 23. 3, Jn. 18. 33, 37); (c) it is explicitly said that Pilate makes an effort to release Jesus (Lk. 22. 16, 20, 22; Jn. 19. 12); [1] (d) the scourging of Jesus is mentioned in a context of his release not his conviction (Lk. 23. 16, 22 b; Jn. 19. 1);[2] (e) a group of Jews comprising not merely the members of the Sanhedrin is mentioned by Pilate as having handed Jesus over to him (Lk. 23. 13 f., Jn. 18. 35); (f) there is evidence, strong enough to convince a number of critics, [3] and which we must therefore examine, that Pilate handed Jesus over to be crucified not to the Roman soldiers but to the Jews; (g) Jesus is explicitly charged with claiming to be a king (Lk. 23. 2c, Jn. 19. 12); (h) mention of who Barabas is occurs only after the Jews demand his release (Lk. 23. 18 f., Jn. 18. 40);

---

[1] Pilate's question in Mk. 15. 9 cannot be said to constitute such an effort: Mark does not say that Pilate attempted to release Jesus, but rather that he asked the Jews if they wished him to do so.

[2] Luke uses the word παιδεύειν which has a wider range of meanings than John's word μαστιγοῦν, but it is clear (so all the commentators and Bauer, *Wörterbuch zum Neuen Testament, ad loc.*) that παιδεύειν here means the same thing as μαστιγοῦν, i. e. "whip, flog, scourge."

[3] Dibelius, *Zeitschrift für die Neutestamentliche Wissenschaft,* 1915, p. 120, and Conzelmann, *op. cit.*, p. 119, nt. 2, in Luke's case, Bertram, *op. cit.*, p. 70 in John's, and Grant, *op. cit.*, p. 299 in both.

(i) the word αἴρειν is used by the crowd in crying for Jesus' destruction (Lk. 23. 18 αἶρε τοῦτον, Jn. 19. 15 ἆρον ἆρον); (j) "crucify" is repeated twice by the hostile crowd (Lk. 23. 21 σταύρου σταύρου, Jn. 19. 6 σταύρωσον σταύρωσον). [1]

The list is a long one; but that it does not tell the whole story is clear from the following list of the differences between the two accounts. In Luke the Jews make a formal charge at the beginning of the trial, which takes place on the day of the Passover festival; Pilate questions Jesus in front of the Jews and, convinced of his innocence, sends him to Herod who, questioning Jesus and receiving no answer, sends him back—whereupon Pilate twice vainly suggests to the Jews that he be scourged and released. In John, according to whom the trial occurs before the Passover feast, Jesus is not questioned by Pilate in front of the Jews but alone inside the *pretorium,* into which the Jews fearing ritual contamination refuse to come; no formal charge is made against Jesus by the Jews; Pilate twice suggests that the Jews themselves deal with Jesus; and Pilate goes back and forth between Jesus and the Jews (the result is that the trial is divided into eight scenes), has Jesus scourged, and twice leads him out of the pretorium and presents him to the Jews.

Due to the number of the agreements between Luke and John and the diversity of the issues they raise, it will be necessary to discuss them one by one. But, because the points of agreement are so closely tied up with the special material each evangelist offers, in order to be in a position adequately to discuss the former we must first examine the latter in order to see whether we find evidence of a written source for either Luke or John from which they may have derived the material they have in common. The material which Luke alone offers, agreeing neither with Mark nor with John, comprises two elements, the charges made against Jesus by the Jews in 23. 2, and Jesus' examination by Herod. As to the first of these, the phraseology and content of the charges points not to Luke's use of a written source but to Lukan compo-

[1] Schniewind, *op. cit.*, p. 69, maintains that in Luke's and John's account, but not in Mark's and Matthew's, the hearing before Pilate constitutes a regular trial, and cites in support Lk. 23. 14 ἐγὼ ἐνώπιον ὑμῶν ἀνακρίνας and Pilate's sitting on the judgment seat in Jn. 19. 13. But he fails to take into account Mk. 15. 15 b παρέδωκεν τὸν Ἰησοῦν φραγγελώσας ἵνα σταυρωθῇ which gives the impression of an official sentence (and therefore the conclusion of a regular trial) far more than Lk. 18. 25b or Jn. 19. 16 do.

sition: τὸ ἔθνος ἡμῶν is found elsewhere in the New Testament only in Lk. 7. 5, and the fact that the second accusation leveled by the Jews directly contradicts what Jesus has said to the very same Jews in Lk. 20. 25 is an indication that this accusation stems from Luke's skilful hand. [1] There is every reason to believe that v. 2 was inserted by Luke in front of v. 3, which he took over from Mark, in order to provide the necessary prelude to Pilate's question to Jesus in v. 3. [2] As for the Herod scene, its content indicates that it too stems not from a written source but from Luke's hand. [3]

---

[1] This is confirmed by the occurrence of φόρος in both Lk. 20. 25 and here in 23. 2, whereas Mark in 12. 13 has κῆνσος.

[2] This is not to say that Luke is composing completely freely in v. 3 (though it is likely that he is responsible not only for the second accusation but for the equation of χριστός and βασιλεύς in the third, this latter serving the purpose of relating the accusation before Pilate to that before the Sanhedrin). For it was common knowledge that Jesus was executed by the Romans as dangerous to them (this follows not only from the content of the trial in Mark but from the known fact that the Romans *had* executed him). Further, if Jesus was executed as a Zealot (so Cullmann, *The State in the New Testament*, pp. 41 ff.) then Luke may very likely have derived the first accusation from a historical tradition. But there is no indication that Luke was dependent here on a written source; he drew, rather, on tradition circulating orally in the Christian community. On the accusation that Jesus was calling himself a king, see below.

[3] That Herod's desire to see Jesus in 23. 8 is a theological motif stemming from Luke is indicated by the insertion of the same motif in 9. 9 where Luke is otherwise following Mark (see Conzelmann, *op. cit.*, p. 89 on "seeing" as one of Luke's theological motifs)—also, ἐξ ἱκανῶν χρόνων in 23. 8 is an expression found elsewhere in the New Testament only in Luke (twice) and Acts (three times). Jesus' refusal to answer in 23. 9 is derived from Mk. 15. 4, which Luke deletes; v. 10 is very similar to Mk. 15. 3, which Luke also deletes, as is v. 11 to Mk. 15. 17 (also deleted). Further, v. 5 also stems from Luke: cf. καθ' ὅλης τῆς Ἰουδαίας ἀρξάμενος ἀπὸ τῆς Γαλιλαίας there and in Acts 10. 37; even if Conzelmann, *op. cit.*, p. 71 is right that we've here a pre-Lucan form, it is unquestionably the evangelist who used it at this point in composing an introduction to the Herod scene. Taylor, *op. cit.*, pp. 52 f., maintains that Luke hasn't constructed the scene but that he's used a source (proto-Luke) which he preferred to Mark, so that he eliminated all parallel Marcan elements; however the strange lack of any new, non-Marcan material in the scene tells heavily against this, as Creed, *op. cit.*, *ad loc.*, and Finegan, *op. cit.*, p. 28, point out. Nevertheless, that is not to say that Luke was the first to conceive an examination of Jesus by Herod, though that the episode is not historical is indicated by the unlikelihood that Pilate would send a political prisoner to be tried by Herod within his own jurisdiction (the apologetic nature of the motif is seen from the development it later undergoes in the apocryphal literature, e.g. in the gospel of Peter, where in v. 2 Herod not Pilate gives the command to crucify Jesus). The conception is due to a Christian interpretation of the first verse of the second psalm (so Dibelius, *op. cit.*, p. 125, Creed *op. cit.*, *ad loc.*, and Bultmann, *op. cit.*, p. 294); it is

As for John's special material, we shall first examine the basic scheme of John's account, that according to which the Jews, because the trial occurred before the Passover, remain outside the *pretorium* and Pilate goes back and forth between them and Jesus. It is at once clear that it is historically unlikely that Pilate examined Jesus not before his accusers but privately; the situation is better explained as a device devised by the evangelist to enable him to expand the account of the trial and provide a more adequate, i.e. more intimate, setting for the Pilate-Jesus dialogues which he constructed. [1] This device is in turn made possible by the chronological scheme according to which the trial day was the fourteenth not the fifteenth of Nisan, which resulted in the Jews' refusal to enter the *pretorium*, lest they be disqualified from participation in the Passover through having entered the house of a Gentile. Have we in this dating a genuine historical tradition taken over by John? The evidence does not point to its historicity. [2] The question

likely that it originated before Luke (so Dibelius, *ibid.*, and Haenchen, *Die Apostelgeschichte*, p. 190), as an element in the oral tradition; Luke, however, in composing his gospel, was the first to write it down, and all the details of his account stem from him.

[1] That he is responsible for these latter in their present form is manifest: 33-37 is an expansion of Lk. 23. 3 f. (on which see further below); for 18. 36 cf. 8. 23, 3. 3, 5; for 18. 37 b cf. 10. 27, 8. 47; for 19. 11a cf. 3. 27, 10. 18. (To say that John has constructed these dialogues in their present form does not exclude John's use here of oral tradition to the effect that Jesus before Pilate stressed the non-political nature of his kingdom, oral tradition which O. Cullmann, *op. cit.*, p. 30, believes to be historically accurate.) Indeed it is likely that Pilate's twice leading Jesus out to the Jews, and indeed the whole scheme whereby Pilate goes back and forth between the Jews and Jesus, was suggested to John by a reading of Mk. 15. 16 ff., where the soldiers—the Jews remaining outside—mock Jesus as a king in the *pretorium* (cf. Jn. 19.2 f.) and he is then led out to be crucified.

[2] The notice that the Jews in entering a Gentile house would through ritual impurification be prevented from participating in the Passover is contradicted by *Pesahim* VII 6, as Barrett, *op. cit.*, p. 444, points out. As to the dating itself, it contradicts the synoptic accounts, according to which Jesus was executed on the fifteenth of Nisan. For the genuineness of the synoptic chronology speaks the fact that all four accounts of the last supper (including John's!) give ample evidence that it was a Passover meal (on this see Jeremias, *The Eucharistic Words of Jesus*, pp. 14-57); further, the argument earlier much employed that the events of the passion cannot have taken place on the day of the feast has been demonstrated as false by Dalman, *op. cit.*, pp. 98 ff., and Barrett, *op. cit.*, pp. 40 f. A. Jaubert, in *La Date de la Cène*, has recently attempted to reconcile the discrepancy between the synoptic chronology and that of John by means of the postulation that Jesus—and following him the synoptic evangelists—used the Jewish solar calendar (whose existence we know of from the book of Jubilees and the Qumran and

must then be asked whether this unhistorical tradition arose with John or was taken over by him from a source, possibly a written one. The fact that as early as Paul (1 Cor. 5. 7) Christ was understood as the Passover lamb—out of which understanding the Johannine dating arose [1]—points up the possibility that already before John a tradition may have arisen according to which Jesus was crucified on the fourteenth of Nisan. Certainty here is not possible. If John was dependent on such a tradition, the fact, as we shall see, that all the other details peculiar to his account stem from him points to its being an isolated oral tradition, not part of an extensive source, much less a written one. On the other hand, it is perhaps on the whole more likely that John, with his strong sense of pneumatic authority, was the first to alter the chronology of the passion in the interest of his Christological interpretation than that this was already done in the oral tradition.

The remaining special material in John's gospel does not point to a special source for the evangelist either, but rather at the most to his use of isolated elements of oral tradition. Pilate's two suggestions that the Jews take Jesus and deal with him on their own (18. 31, 19. 6b), the fancifulness of which is clear enough

---

Damascus Sect writings) according to which the Passover was reckoned to fall on Wednesday (beginning Tuesday at sunset), whereas the fourth evangelist followed the ultimately prevailing lunar calendar in reckoning the Passover to fall on Friday. According to Jaubert's reconstruction, in historical fact Jesus after celebrating the Passover with his disciples on Tuesday evening was arrested that night but not executed until Friday. But Miss Jaubert fails to explain how all four evangelists came to telescope the arrest-trial-crucifixion events into one day, or how the fourth evangelist, whom she believes to have been the beloved disciple, came to adopt the lunar calendar in relation to events which he himself, as a participant in them, knew to have been reckoned by Jesus and all the participants according to the solar calendar—i. e. how he came to displace the celebration of the Passover feast. Her thesis, therefore, is not convincing.

[1] It was inferred that, if Christ was the Passover lamb, he must have died the same day the lamb was always slaughtered, i. e. the fourteenth of Nisan. That John affirmed the interpretation of Christ as the lamb is clear from 1. 29 and 19. 36, and that it molded his account of the Passion is confirmed by the fact that John notes in 19. 14, as the other evangelists do not, that Jesus was condemned (i. e. offered up to the will of the Jews) by Pilate in the sixth hour, the hour at which the Passover lamb was slaughtered; Bacon, *The Fourth Gospel in Research and Debate*, p. 421, thinks further that the explanation of the dating of Jn. 12. 11 ff. is that it identifies the day as the tenth of Nisan, that on which (see Exodus 12. 3) the Passover lamb was chosen.

from the content of the second, [1] surely originated with John. The detail that Barabbas was a thief (18. 40) is a mistake on John's part; he has confused him with the two men crucified with Jesus whom Mark describes as thieves but whom he John doesn't describe at all. [2] The detail that Pilate sat on a judgment seat before handing down sentence does not require the postulation of a source; the judgment seat is mentioned by Mt. 27. 19, and the evangelist surely knew anyway of the custom of using such a seat since a sentence was always handed down by a judge so seated. [3] Finally, the location of the trial in Gabbatha will have been known to John from oral tradition. [4]

We have now examined both the material peculiar to Luke and that peculiar to John and have determined that for neither do we find evidence of the use of more than fragments of oral tradition. We may therefore go on to discuss the elements on which they agree, assured that the other elements in both pericopes do not point to extensive sources for the evangelists at this point, and that we are only justified in assuming such if the evidence of the elements on which they agree points to it.

We shall discuss first the most striking agreement, the threefold statement of Pilate. As far as its appearance in Luke is concerned, did it originate with the evangelist, or did he derive it

---

[1] There is no indication that Pilate is being ironic in his suggestion that the Jews do the impossible, i. e. carry out an execution in the Roman manner.

[2] So correctly Finegan, *op. cit.*, p. 46. The meaning "guerilla" for ληστής, suggsteed by Barrett, *op. cit.*, *ad loc.* — which, if accepted, would mean that John doesn't differ from the synoptics—is too secondary to be here correct.

[3] So Schürer, *op. cit.*, 4th ed., I, p. 429, nt. 8.

[4] Bultmann, *Das Evangelium des Johannes*, *ad loc.*, on the basis of the problematical πάλιν in 18. 40—problematical because the crowd has not previously cried out—sees John as utilizing a written source in which the crowd had immediately previously cried out requesting Barabbas' release. This source he sees as closely parallel to the synoptic accounts, containing among other elements the Barabbas incident, the mention of Gabbatha and a statement by Pilate of Jesus' innocence; the shifting of scenes and the chronology he attributes to the evangelist. But πάλιν here may, like the Aramaic מוב, have the meaning "then, thereupon," as Klostermann, *op. cit.*, *ad loc.*, suggests. Or it may refer back—if ineptly—to vv. 29-32 (so Windisch, *op. cit.*, p. 84); or John may here be echoing Luke, where the analogous verse, 23. 18, is preceded by 23. 5 (so Goguel, *op. cit.*, p. 381). We cannot be certain which is correct. But it is surely as unjustified to construct an elaborate source theory for John on the basis of πάλιν in 18. 40 as it would be to do so for Mark's trial account on the basis of the equally problematical πάλιν in Mk. 15. 13.

from a source? Both its content and its form point to the former. In content it is in excellent accord with Luke's theology, according to which the Jews were alone responsible for Jesus' death (e.g. Acts 3. 15, 4. 10, 5. 30, 10. 39), and in its (three-fold) form it is admirably adapted to produce a dramatic scene of the kind Luke liked (cf. his account of Peter's denial). It is true, as Dibelius has seen, [1] that Pilate's statement in v. 4 is confusing, coming so abruptly on top of v. 3; this remains the case even if, with Grant, [2] one sees Luke as having understood Jesus' σὺ λέγεις in v. 3 to mean simply "yes." [3] This can be explained on the ground that Luke, using Mark, composed the scene as he did in order to make room for three statements of Jesus' innocence on Pilate's part, even at the price of having the first occur rather precipitately. It can, to be sure, also be explained on the basis that Luke had a source in which the three-fold statement occurred, and that he is, rather unevenly, fitting the two together. [4] But, in that case, what was the content of the source beyond Pilate's statements? The second of these statements does not result from further examination of Jesus on Pilate's part but from the examination by Herod, which as we saw stems in its present form from Luke's pen; indeed 15a, related to Pilate's first and second statements as it is, gives the reason for the inclusion of the Herod incident in Luke's gospel. Here, in the connection between the three-fold statement and the Herod scene, we see further, indeed decisive, evidence of the former as stemming from the evangelist not a source. [5]

John as we know knew Luke's gospel; the simplest and most satisfactory explanation of the three-fold statement in his gospel is that he was sufficiently impressed by it when he encountered it in Luke to incorporate it into his gospel, using as the model of all three of the statements in his gospel the first, unqualified statement of innocence occurring in Luke (23. 4). Only so is the marked similarity between the vocabulary of his statements and

[1] Dibelius, *op. cit.*, p. 119.

[2] Grant, *op. cit.*, p. 298.

[3] In view of the fact that σὺ λέγεις in Mk. 15. 2, whence Luke derived it, certainly does not have this simple negative meannig, it is by no means certain that it does in Luke, even though the assumption that it does reduces the difficulty in vv. 3 f.

[4] So Bertram, *op. cit.*, p. 65.

[5] The notion that Pilate knew Jesus was innocent did not originate with Luke; it occurs already in Mark (15. 10), whence Luke derived it. What is new with Luke is the emphasis on the point.

those in Luke explicable.[1] [2] Pilate's belief in Jesus' innocence is, in fact, even clearer in John than in Luke. This is due not only to the unqualified form of all Pilate's statements as he reports them, but to the fact that by means of the two discourses between Jesus and Pilate which he relates (18. 35-38a, 19. 9b-11) John explains *why* Pilate knew that Jesus was innocent; these dialogues represent John's development of the three-fold Pilate statement he took over from Luke. This development is seen most clearly in Jn. 18. 33-38, which is an expansion of Lk. 23. 3 f.[3] This is one of the very few instances in John where in composing a discourse on the basis of a passage from one of the synoptic gospels the fourth evangelist remained so close to his source that we can discern with certainty the tradition as he found it and the material which he added to it. However, the relationship between Luke and John here is not so simple as it at first seems. As we saw above, the interpretation of σὺ λέγεις in Lk. 23. 3 which reduces to a minimum the abruptness of that verse is that according to which it means "no"; but that

---

[1] John's only significant departure from Luke in this regard is his use in all three statements of αἰτία rather than αἴτιον which Luke uses. (D's reading of αἰτία in Lk. 23. 22 is clearly secondary, reflecting the influence of the Johannine text.) Zurhellen, *op. cit.*, p. 51, followed by Schniewind, *op. cit.*, p. 69, thinks that the three-fold statements in Luke and John do not demonstrate a direct knowledge of Luke by John, Zurhellen holding the view that we have two parallel, unconnected products of a similar apologetic interest, Schniewind that a common oral tradition lay behind both. But these possibilities are excluded by the virtual identity of the first of the three statements in the two gospels. Grant, *op. cit.*, p. 298, thinks that John can't have known the Lucan pericope because if he had he'd have taken over or anyway hinted at the Herod scene which would have been so acceptable to him theologically; he therefore postulates that the Pilate statements in Luke are glosses representing late Johannine influence on the Lucan text. But there is no manuscript evidence for this hypothesis; furthermore the first of the statements, in v. 4, is the necessary link between vv. 3 and 5; without it, the context cannot stand. There is, in fact, no necessity for Grant's hypothesis, as the argument *e silentio* from which it follows doesn't stand up against the positive evidence, here and elsewhere, that John knew Luke's gospel.

[2] Schniewind believes that further parallels can be demonstrated between Luke's and John's structure beyond that of the threefold Pilate statement. But his efforts, *op. cit.*, pp. 62 ff., to demonstrate these are unsuccessful, due to the fact that in Luke the Herod scene intervenes between the first and second Pilate statements, and the Barabbas incident issues from the second statement, whereas in John the Barabbas incident arises out of the first Herod statement, and the scourging and *ecce homo* scene intervene between the second and third Pilate statements.

[3] So already H. J. Holtzmann, *op. cit.*, p. 79.

Jesus with σὺ λέγεις in Jn. 18. 37 meant "no", i.e. that he denied his kingship, is excluded by v. 36, and 19.14b, 15 and 22 show that Pilate did not understand Jesus to mean "no" with this answer. John has, therefore, not merely set out to explain, to provide a commentary, on what he found in Luke, he has transformed Luke's content. [1]

In discussing Pilate's attempt to release Jesus in Luke and John, it will be convenient to deal first with the scourging which in both gospels is associated with this attempt. The matter of the scourging differs from that of Pilate's statements of Jesus' innocence in that John goes beyond Luke in what he reports. i.e. the scourging which is merely suggested in Luke actually occurs in John. [2] Have we, then, a Johannine tradition here, mirrored in partial form in Luke—a tradition which is possibly historical? Before answering we must be clear as to the meaning of the scourging in the two passages. In Luke Pilate's suggestion that he scourge and release Jesus (23. 16 and 23. 22) both times follow declarations that he finds Jesus innocent of any capital offense; if the qualification θανάτου in these declarations is to be taken at face value, then the meaning must be that Pilate finds Jesus guilty of a minor offense, and so suggests scourging as an adequate punishment. However, since Pilate's first statement in 23. 4 is a statement of Jesus' unqualified innocence, and this finding of Pilate's is referred to and reaffirmed by him in v. 14 just before he makes the second statement of innocence and the scourging suggestion which follows it, it must be that θανάτου in this second statement (v. 15), and in the third (v. 22) has no real significance, and that Pilate's suggestion of scourging is a suggestion of compromise, compromise between the Jews' desire for Jesus' destruction and Pilate's own conviction that he merits no punishment whatever. In John, Pilate's scourging of Jesus represents an effort on his part to save the life of a man whom he believes to be innocent by satisfying the Jews with a minor punishment, i.e. his leading

[1] Schniewind's comment, therefore, *op. cit.*, p. 63, that Lk. 23. 3 f. is ununderstandable without Jn. 18. 33-38, is incorrect. For John does not simply mean the same thing, in expanded, clarified form, that Luke does; though, or rather just because, he is seeking to interpret the Christian (here specifically the Lucan) tradition so as to produce a profound clarification of it, he has not merely echoed his source; his version explains his view, not Luke's; our ability to understand Luke is not thereby affected.

[2] It also occurs in Mark and Matthew, but in a different context.

Jesus forth scourged and crowned with thorns and with a purple gown represents an effort to make Jesus seem laughable and sufficiently punished, to get the case laughed out of court. [1]

The proceeding in both Luke and John is problematical because we've no record of a parallel use of scourging on the part of a Roman judge. On the other hand what Mark (in 15.15) and Matthew (in 27. 26) report, that Pilate had Jesus scourged as a preliminary to crucifixion, is attested as a Roman custom by Josephus and Livy. [2] Because of this it's not justified to see in the Lucan-Johannine tradition one which can lay legitimate claim to historicity. We must still determine whether it originated with Luke and was taken over by John, or whether, as in the case of Jesus' serving at the last supper Luke echoes a Johannine tradition here. The former is here the simpler and more satisfactory explanation. The scourging suggestion came into being in Luke because the evangelist saw Mk. 15. 15-20 as integrally related to φραγγελώσας in Mk. 15. 15, indeed as comprising a description of the events centering about the scourging. When he dropped Mk. 15. 16-20 from his account, [3] he therefore dropped the mention of scourging immediately preceding it, or rather he used the element elsewhere, in the form of a suggestion, as part of the theme of Pilate's effort to obtain Jesus' release, a theme suggested to him by Mk. 15. 9. [4] John, on reading Luke, was struck by the occurrence of the scourging suggestion in a context of Pilate's seeking Jesus' release; he transformed the suggestion into an act, using it in the complex of events leading up to and constituting the *ecce homo* scene. [5]

The question remains whether it is historical that Pilate made

---

[1] It is, to be sure, not explicitly said that the scourging and leading forth of Jesus have this purpose, and indeed this interpretation appears to be excluded by 19. 12, which states that only after Pilate's second discourse with Jesus did Pilate seek Jesus' release. But we must assume that John is expressing himself inexactly in 19. 12, for if one takes that verse at face value it deprives both the scourging and the *ecce homo* scene of all meaning.

[2] Josephus, *De Bello Iudaico*, II 308, V 449; Livy, *Ab Urbe Condita*, XXXIII 36.

[3] On why he did so see below.

[4] In Luke the scourging remains a suggestion because the release of Jesus advocated by Pilate, with which it is bound up, also remains merely a suggestion.

[5] That John subordinated the scourging element to the *ecce homo* scene, using it to increase the drama and power of the latter, explains why he located the scourging inside the *pretorium* and not, as one would expect if its purpose was to satisfy the Jews' desire for blood, outside it, in front of them.

any effort at all to release Jesus, as, quite apart from the scourging, Luke in 23. 20 and John in 19. 12 report. Oscar Cullmann [1] thinks that Pilate's reluctance to pronounce the death sentence may be historical, explicable on the ground that Pilate saw that Jesus was politically innocuous. In view of the pictures of Jesus' activity which we have from the sources (i.e. the gospels) this is very likely. But that is a different matter from Pilate's actively interceding in Jesus' behalf, and it is doubtful if either Lk. 23. 20 or Jn. 19. 12 can be considered to reflect historically reliable information. Luke, in 23. 20 as in Pilate's suggestions that he release Jesus in 23. 16 and 23. 22b, was motivated by the desire to absolve Pilate of all responsibility for Jesus' death; it is most unlikely that he had any source here beyond Mark. And John in 19. 12 is in all likelihood following Luke. [2]

Next to be discussed are Pilate's statements that not merely the Jewish leaders, members of the Sanhedrin, but also a λάος (Lk. 23. 13 f.) or τὸ ἔθνος τὸ σόν (Jn. 18. 35) had brought Jesus to him. As we shall see, the agreement is more apparent than real; first, however, it should be made clear that on close examination of its context this detail in Luke is seen to have originated with him not with a source. In the Marcan account of the trial which Luke used as a source an unevenness exists in that in the first part of the trial (Mk. 15. 2-5) only the members of the Sanhedrin are present (v. 1), whereas in the second part, which begins with the Barabbas incident, and issues in the pronouncement of the sentence, a crowd is suddenly mentioned as being present (v. 11), without any explanation of how it got there—there having been no indication of change of scene. [3] In Luke's pericope, despite the insertion of the Herod scene in between, the trial before Pilate consists of these same two parts. 27. 13 represents the beginning

[1] Cullmann, *op. cit.* pp. 46 f.

[2] The case is different, however, with Mk. 15. 9 f., 14 a, which may be accepted as substantially historical; these verses, however, are more circumspect in describing Pilate's efforts on Jesus' behalf—i. e. in 9, as pointed out above, Pilate does not say he wishes to release Jesus but asks the Jews whether it is their wish.

[3] Mark specifically distinguishes (v. 11) between the crowd and the chief-priests (by whom he presumably, speaking loosely, means all the members of the Sanhedrin), and it is the presence of the crowd which gives point to Pilate's question as to whom the Jews wish released. For the question would make no sense if only the Jews who had specifically requested Jesus' execution were there when Pilate asked if they wanted him released.

of the second part, that highlighted by mention of Barabbas. Luke, following Mark, has not mentioned a crowd previously, but, again following Mark, he records its presence in the Barabbas scene. To do so, avoiding the unevenness of Mark's account, and at the same time provide the continuity of audience on which Pilate's statement in Lk. 23. 14-16 depends, Luke (in v. 14) makes their presence retroactive; Pilate says that the crowd, as well as the high priests and rulers, brought Jesus to him, though the crowd is not mentioned in 23. 1. [1] As for John, it is unlikely that in 18.35 he reflects a reading of Lk. 23. 13. [2] For the word he uses there is not λαός (the word employed by Luke) or ὄχλος (Mark's term) but ἔθνος; this word can mean "company, body of men," but the fact that John says here τὸ ἔθνος τὸ σόν excludes this possibility, and assures its having the meaning here which it always has elsewhere in the New Testament (e.g. Jn. 11. 48 ff.), i.e. "race, nation, people." Pilate does not say to Jesus that a specific company of Jews brought Jesus to him, but the Jewish people as a whole. [3] τὸ ἔθνος τὸ σόν means, in fact, the same thing as οἱ 'Ιουδαίοι, the term which John, in 18. 31, 38, 19. 6 f., 12, 14 uses to designate those opposed to Jesus at the trial; the use of ἔθνος does not stem from a synoptic or any other source, but is due to its adequacy to express John's theology. [4]

It is maintained that according to both Luke's and John's accounts it is the Jews and not the Romans who carry out the crucifixion. [5] Support for this view as far as Luke is concerned is to be found in his omission of Mk. 15. 20b, which records that the Roman soldiers lead Jesus out to crucify him. Luke in fact nowhere states explicitly that Roman soldiers crucified Jesus. In 23. 26 ff. the actors are an undefined "they"; it is true that

[1] ἅπαν τὸ πλῆθος there may not be taken as implying the presence of a crowd, as ἀναστάν in the same verse clearly marks this group as one consisting of members of the Sanhedrin.

[2] In 18. 28 John says that "they" brought Jesus from Caiaphas to the pretorium, which "they" probably refers back to the σπεῖρα καὶ ὁ χιλίαρχος καὶ οἱ ὑπηρέται τῶν 'Ιουδαίων referred to in v. 18. 12 as those seizing Jesus at the time of his arrest.

[3] That τὸ ἔθνος τὸ σόν is coupled with οἱ ἀρχιερεῖς does not then mean that John is referring to two groups of Jews, but rather that the chiefpriests are here seen as representative of the Jewish nation.

[4] No support, then, in either Luke or John is to be found for Schniewind's view, *op. cit.*, p. 70, that a common oral tradition lies behind Luke and John whereby not merely the Sanhedrin but crowds brought Jesus to Pilate.

[5] For the proponents of this view see p. 64, nt. 3.

the Jews are the last group to have been mentioned (in 25b), but due to the form of this mention—the verse states that Pilate gave Jesus up, or over, to the *will* of the Jews—it cannot be said to establish the identity of the "they" of vv. 24 ff. as Jews. Furthermore, Roman soldiers are mentioned by Luke as present at the crucifixion, in 23. 36, 47, [1] and in 23. 52 Jesus' body is mentioned as in Pilate's possession. It appears from all this that Luke was content to leave the matter in obscurity. He was determined not specifically to describe the Romans as Jesus' crucifiers; [2] it is likely that he was prevented from doing more than hint that it was the Jews who filled this rôle by the widespread knowledge that any execution the Jews carried out could only taken the form of stoning. [3] As for John, the evangelist states in 19. 16 that Pilate gave Jesus up to the Jews in order that he be crucified. [4] John is probably echoing Lk. 23. 25b, producing a statement which even more than Luke's points to the Jews as responsible for Jesus' death. [5] But that he wished 19. 16 to be taken literally is excluded by 19. 23a, which states that the soldiers crucified Jesus.

As for the Jews' accusation that Jesus claimed to be king, there is no need to postulate either a special source for Luke here, or John's dependence on Luke. That this was the charge made to Pilate against Jesus was clear to Luke from Mk. 15. 2; he inserted it into 23. 2 as the second of the three accusations so as to make Pilate's question in Lk. 23. 3 understandable (as it is not in Mk. 15. 2a). And John hardly needed to draw on Luke for such a generally known fact—known not only from Mark's trial account but from the words written above the cross.

In both Luke and John, Barabbas is first mentioned by the Jews demanding that he and not Jesus be released, and only afterwards is mention made of who he is. Luke, in whose gospel the reference is still more abrupt due to the absense of any introductory note on the custom of releasing a prisoner at the time of

[1] It is not clear how Wellhausen, *Einleitung in die drei ersten Evangelien*, p. 56, and Conzelmann, *op. cit.*, p. 73, nt. 2, can deny this fact.

[2] Cf. Acts 3. 15, 4. 10, 5. 30, 10. 39.

[3] For this reason, quite apart from Mark's and—see below— John's evidence, there can be no question of the Jews having actually, historically, carried out Pilate's sentence.

[4] That αὐτοῖς refers to the Jews is clear from the preceding verses.

[5] That he is here echoing Luke is further indicated by the fact that like Luke he does not record the mocking of Jesus by the Roman soldiers as ensuing at this point.

the festival,[1] seems for the sake of providing a dramatic account to have been willing to provide a somewhat uneven one; the peculiarity here as over against Mark is a purely stylistic one. John in 18. 40 unconsciously took over this single dramatic element from Luke.[2] That he was struck by Lk. 23. 18 is indicated by his adoption of αἶρε τοῦτον from that verse (this use of αἴρειν is characteristically Lucan, being found elsewhere in the New Testament only in Acts 21. 36 and 22. 22, and is used by Luke in 23. 18 in order to increase the drama of his account)in the ἆρον ἆρον . . . αὐτόν of 19. 15.

Finally, the two-fold repetition of "crucify" by the hostile crowd in Lk. 23. 21 is due to Luke's heightening the drama of Mark's account, and John, though he uses the aorist form and not the present, is doubtless echoing Luke here.

Therewith the analysis of the elements common to Luke's and John's Pilate pericopes is complete. We have seen that, where agreements in fact exist, the explanation of them lies not in a special written or oral source used by both, but rather that John has followed the emendations which, on theological or stylistic grounds, Luke has made in Mark's account. On only one point, the charge against Jesus that he claimed to be a king, was there no need to postulate John's dependence on Luke.

---

[1] V. 17, as its absence from A B a and its varying position in the manuscripts which do bring it show, is secondary.

[2] He is, however, in 18. 39 f. closer to Mark than to Luke, as is shown by the introductory mention of the release custom in 18. 39 and the question βούλεσθε οὖν ἀπολύσω ὑμῖν τὸν βασιλέα τῶν Ἰουδαίων in the same verse.

CHAPTER ELEVEN

JESUS' CRUCIFIXION, DEATH AND BURIAL

Luke 23. 25-56 / John 19. 17-42

In their accounts of Jesus' crucifixion, death and burial Luke and John have the following points in common: 1) the statement that two other men were crucified with him follows immediately after the mention of Jesus' crucifixion (Lk. 23. 33, Jn. 19. 18); 2) εἱστήκεισαν is used of the women (in Luke they are part of a larger group) who watch Jesus on the cross (Lk. 23. 49, Jn. 19. 25); 3) both Luke and John have the statement that no one had ever used the tomb (Lk. 23. 53: οὗ οὐκ ἦν οὐδεὶς οὔπω κείμενος, Jn. 19. 41: ἐν ᾧ οὐδέπω οὐδεὶς ἦν τεθειμένος) followed by the statement that that day was the day of Preparation for the Sabbath. Further, a number of negative agreements exist. Neither gospel records the giving to Jesus of wine mixed with myrrh, nor the mocking reference of the bystanders to Jesus' alleged statement that he would destroy the temple, nor Jesus' cry "My God, my God, why hast thou forsaken me?" nor the sealing of the tomb with a stone [1]— though this last is later presupposed in both gospels (Lk. 24. 2, Jn. 20. 1).[2]

[1] The readings of D c sa and of U Φ in Lk 23. 53 are clearly secondary.

[2] Schniewind, *op. cit.*, p. 79, alleges that a common Semitic source for Luke and John is revealed by the way they mention the place of the crucifixion. But this is not correct. All they have in common is the fact that κρανίον is the first designation of the place, not preceded as in Mark and Matthew by Γολγοθᾶ; this is true of Luke because, as is his custom, he contents himself with giving the Greek name, whereas John, in his usual fashion (cf. 5.2, 19. 13), mentions the Hebrew name after the Greek one; there is, that is to say, no connection between them at this point. Schniewind (*op. cit.*, p. 81) further cites the agreement between the two on the point of the materials for the anointing of Jesus' body having been prepared before the Sabbath (Lk. 23. 56, Jn. 19. 40). But Luke records that they were prepared by the women, whose intention (never carried out) was to use them the day after the Sabbath, whereas John records that Nicodemus brought the material the day before the Sabbath and that he and Joseph immediately anointed Jesus with it; there is no connection between the two accounts here, either.

John records (19. 20) that the epigraph placed above the cross was written in Hebrew, Latin and Greek. In Lk. 23. 38 ℵ D θ 𝔎 latt sy[p] record the same fact, though the languages are mentioned in reverse order; 𝔅 a sy[sc] do not bring this. If the reading is genuine, there is an agreement with John, and those manuscripts not bringing it must have left it out through the influence

As usual, an adequate picture of the two accounts in relation to one another requires a listing of the points at which they diverge. Luke records three statements of Jesus from the cross, [1] John three quite different ones! Luke records that Simon Cyrene carried the cross, further a prophetic statement of Jesus to the grieving women uttered on his way to Golgotha, the mocking of Jesus by the Jewish rulers and soldiers, the differing reactions to him of the two criminals crucified with him, the splitting of the veil of the temple and the reaction of the centurion to his death. John records that Jesus carried his own cross, that his garment was seamless—further, the incident of Pilate's insisting on the wording of the superscription, the bone-breaking incident, the spearing of Jesus' side, Nicodemus' participation in the annointing and burial, the occurrence of the annointing before the Sabbath, and the burial of Jesus in a garden. [2]

It is clear when one analyzes the Lucan and Johannine pericopes that the evidence does not point to a common source, written or oral, for the two here. That Luke used Mark as the foundation of his account is indicated by the occurrence in his gospel, substantially unaltered, of the Marcan skeleton of events: mention of Simon carrying the cross, of the name of the place of crucifixion, of the parting of the garments, the mocking, the reproach of both (or one) of the criminals, the darkness from the sixth to the ninth hour, Jesus' death, the centurion's reaction, the Galilean women watching, the rôle of Joseph of Arimathea and the burial; this, combined with Luke's verbal similarities to Mark in 12. 44 and 12. 51 f., constitutes conclusive evidence of Luke's use of Mark. At five places, to be sure, Luke's order is different from Mark's: (a) the crucified evildoers are mentioned by Luke before not after

of Matthew and Mark; if it is not genuine, then it indicates a late Johannine influence on the Lucan text. The fact of the unlikelihood of Mark's and Matthew's having had such a strong, negative influence on the Lucan text, plus the divergencies among the readings offered by the Lucan texts which bring the statement, point to the latter. The fact that the order of languages mentioned in the Lucan manuscripts is different from that in John presents no problem to this view, for the Lucan order is the one which was usual (cf. the citations of imperial proclamations in Bauer, *Das Johannesevangelium, ad loc.*) and represents a correction of the Johannine text from which it was derived.

[1] On whether the first of these constitutes an original part of Luke's text see below.

[2] The list of women present at the crucifixion in Luke and in John agree only where they also agree with Mark, as there is no justification for identifying Joanna (Lk. 24. 10) with Jesus' aunt (Jn. 19. 25).

the parting of the garments; (b) the superscription is mentioned in the midst of the mocking of Jesus, not before it; (c) the giving of vinegar to Jesus occurs before not after the mention of the darkness; (d) the veil splits before Jesus' death, not after; and (e) the mention of the date occurs after the burial not before it. All five, however, are to be explained on the basis of Luke's editorial action. The first represents Luke's effort to produce an account more unified than Mark's, where the two thieves are somewhat belatedly mentioned; the second and third occur owing to the fact that Luke understands both the superscription and the giving of vinegar as instances of the mocking of Jesus by his tormentors, and so places them with the other instances of mocking; the fourth stems from Luke's uniting the (in Mark separate) elements of the darkness and the splitting of the veil, and placing both before, building up to, the climax of Jesus' death—which event, not as in Mark the veil's splitting, causes the centurion's reaction; the fifth is due to Luke's desire to mention the date by way of introduction to vv. 55 f., whose purpose is to explain that, and why, the women waited until Sunday before visiting the tomb. [1]

However, Luke, though he used Mark, was not satisfied with Mark's depiction of the scene of Christ on the cross, the event which was so scandalous, so difficult for Christians to understand. He was concerned to show that, going to and even on the cross, Jesus was not passive, not despairing, but active and confident to the end. To this purpose he eliminated Jesus' cry "My God, my God," [2] and introduced non-Marcan material into his account: Jesus' speech to the grieving women following him to Golgotha,

---

[1] Schniewind, *op. cit.*, p. 80, following B. Weiss, *Die Evangelien des Markus und Lukas*, p. 676, maintains that in v. 55 f. (where the women do not hesitate to prepare the anointing materials on the day of Jesus' death, but "rest according to the commandment" the following day, the Sabbath) we have a tradition according to which the day of Jesus' death didn't have Sabbath character, i.e. wasn't the Passover; he therefore finds here a tradition agreeing with the fourth gospel dating of events. This is, however, reading too much into of the text; in vv. 55 f. Luke is reworking Mark; his purpose is to explain that (and in v. 56 why) the women waited till Sunday to visit the tomb; the incongruity of their actions on the Passover and the Sabbath, due to his placing the preparation of the materials on Friday not Sunday, didn't occur to him.

[2] Whatever Mark may have understood by these words, Luke's elimination of them shows that he did not understand them as an utterance of confidence.

the words from the cross, and the mocking of the soldiers.[1] He made other changes in Mark too. He omitted the giving to Jesus of wine mixed with myrrh, because he regarded it as a doublet of the giving of vinegar. He did not record the mockers' ironic reference to the temple, for in his opinion the statement about Jesus' destroying the temple belonged no more here than in Jesus' hearing before the high priest, but rather in connection with Stephen's martyrdom (Acts 6. 14). At several points Luke took pains to bring out the fact that the events recorded constituted fulfilments of Old Testament prophecy, as in v. 49, where he added εἱστήκεισαν and οἱ γνωστοί to Mk. 15. 40, which already contained the words ἀπὸ μακρόθεν, in order to bring out the connection with Ps. 37. 12 and 87. 9 (LXX). As for Luke's failure to mention Joseph's rolling a stone before the tomb entrance, it stems perhaps from an unconscious effort on Luke's part to reduce the obviousness of the problem of how the women, knowing the stone to have been placed there, could nevertheless go to the tomb two days later with the clear intention of gaining access to Jesus' body.

John as much as Luke was dissatisfied with Mark's account of events; he shared with Luke a desire to present the scene in such a manner as to bring out the fact that Jesus, in dying, did so voluntarily, without turmoil, confident in the knowledge that in dying he was fulfilling his mission. That John did not come to this view only through an acquaintance with Luke's gospel is shown by such statements in his gospel as 8. 29, 10. 18 and 16. 32. However, because of the very conformity of Luke's account to his own views he was considerably influenced by it. Though he replaced Mark's "My God, my God, why hast thou forsaken me?" with "It is finished" rather than Luke's "Into thy hands I deliver my spirit," there is every reason to think that John was following Luke's example in his elimination of the Marcan statement from Jesus' mouth.[2] So too John uses as the expression for Jesus' dying

[1] That is not to say that the material Luke added to the pericope originated with him. The speech of Jesus to the grieving women, for instance, gives every sign of being pre-Lucan. Of the three words from the cross, the third appears to stem from Luke, who (cf. Acts 7. 59) constructed it to replace the unacceptable Marcan word. As for the first, it is possible that it had nothing to do with the original Lucan gospel but is, as Joachim Jeremias (in a seminar in Göttingen in 1957) has suggested, an authentic word of Jesus, an *agraphon* which penetrated about 100 AD into a number of Lucan manuscripts.

[2] John was, characteristically, more drastic in his measures than Luke. Whereas Luke retained Jesus' last cry (from Mk 15. 34), but altered its

παραδιδόναι τὸ πνεῦμα;[1] in view of the element of volition expressed by the word παραδιδόναι it is apparent that John is here echoing Jesus' last word from Luke.[2] It is true that John is independent of Luke in the words he records Jesus as having said from the cross. At this point of supreme importance, confident, as 14. 26 shows, in his (and every Christian's!) Spirit-given knowledge of the words which Jesus spoke, he goes his own way. But that he was nevertheless struck by Luke's account is clear from the number of relatively unimportant points at which he follows him. So the note in 19. 41 that the tomb had never been used, though in vocabulary varying somewhat from Luke's, is sufficiently similar to it[3] to ensure that John is here following Luke. Also, in the lack of mention both of wine mixed with myrrh and the sealing of the tomb, John reflects Luke.[4] Further, John reflects Luke's order

character by associating it with the statement "Father, into your hands I deliver my spirit," John eliminated the cry entirely.

[1] Mark and following him Luke use ἐξέπνευσεν, Matthew has ἀφῆκεν τὸ πνεῦμα—both neutral expressions. Barrett, *op. cit.*, *ad loc.*, points out that despite Jn. 7. 39 which might seem to point to it, the expression παρέδωκεν τὸ πνεῦμα in 19.30 cannot refer to Jesus' imparting of the Spirit, because that occurs in 20. 23.

[2] So correctly Barrett, *op. cit.*, *ad loc.* Bultmann, *op. cit.*, *ad loc.*, maintains that there can be no connection between Luke and John here because of the absence of the words εἰς χεῖρας from John's text; but this is to fail to perceive that here as often where he did not follow him slavishly John was influenced by Luke.

[3] Barrett, *op. cit.*, *ad loc.*, points out the "ugly collation of sounds" in both the Lucan and Johannine phrases.

[4] It is admittedly a strange coincidence that neither Luke nor John records the sealing of the tomb, though both presuppose it. This phenomenon causes Spitta, *Die Auferstehung Christi* pp. 34 ff., to maintain that neither Luke nor John know of a sealed tomb, and that the mention of a stone in Lk. 24. 2 and Jn. 20. 1 is due in both cases to secondary interpolation under the influence of the Marcan and Matthean text. Spitta believes, moreover, that this tradition (which he thinks Luke and John independently of one another offer), according to which the tomb was not sealed, is the historical one, and explains why the women were able to go to the tomb on Sunday morning expecting to enter it. This hypothesis cannot stand the test of criticism. Luke in 23. 53, as a comparison of that verse with Mk. 15. 46 makes clear, is following Mark; there is no evidence at all of his use of a non-Marcan tradition at this point. As for John, though in the account of the burial he departs from Luke at a number of points (e. g. the presence of Nicodemus, the anointing of Jesus on the day of his death), he follows him, as we've seen, just at the point of describing the tomb—so in all likelihood he also does so in his omission of an account of its sealing. Further, there is no manuscript evidence of additions to Lk. 24. 2 and Jn. 20. 1. We have, to be sure, evidence of late additions to the Lucan text as regards the stone, i. e. the mention of the sealing of the tomb in the D c sa and U Φ

of events at two points: in regard to the mention of the crucifixion of the two others immediately after mention of Jesus' crucifixion,[1] and in the mention of Jesus' burial in a new tomb. Though these are two isolated points, it's significant that by contrast John never once follows Mark's order. This reflects the fact that here, as uniformly throughout the account of the passion, John was more impressed by Luke's account than by Mark's, and hence used him more—though John's partial independence at this point of Luke as well as Mark shouldn't be lost sight of.[2] The matter of the absence in John of the mocking reference to the temple represents quite a different case. John recounts no mocking of Jesus on the cross at all, excluding it on the ground that it was unbecoming at the time of what was at once Jesus' crucifixion and his glorification. Luke, on the other hand, gives a fuller account of the mocking of Jesus than either Mark or Matthew does, despite his omission of the one detail. John's omission here has nothing to do with Luke's; at this point the two go in opposite directions. As for the εἱστήκεισαν in 19. 25, it is so small a detail that in all likelihood the agreement with Luke is purely coincidental.

There remains one point to discuss. John records, departing from the synoptics, that Jesus on the way to Golgotha carried his

---

mss. of 23. 53; and this very fact should make us cautious in assuming that changes have been made in the very first, the original manuscript of the gospel, or rather of both gospels(!); such additions by a later hand would in all likelihood have occurred in a copy of the original manuscript and so, like the Lk. 23. 53 additions, been found only in some of the manuscripts, not in all.

[1] Luke, to be sure, also mentions the two to be crucified earlier, before their crucifixion actually occurs (23. 32), as John does not.

[2] Bultmann, *op. cit.*, *ad loc.*, accounts for John's special material (or all of it except Pilate's insistence on the wording of the inscription, Jesus' word to his mother and the beloved disciple, and the blood-and-water mention) on the basis of John's use of a written source. But, aside from the fact that there is no way to demonstrate this (Bultmann's method of distinguishing between what belonged in the source and what John added is to isolate the elements which appear to him to be particularly "Johannine" and attribute them to the evangelist), it is not a satisfactory procedure. No room is left at all for John as a gatherer of elements of oral tradition, nor for John as drawing on, as well as reacting against, the only previous written sources we can be sure he knew, i. e. the Marcan and Lucan gospels; as we've seen, it is not necessary to fall back on Bultmann's catch-all solution to the problem of John's contents to explain either his omission of the Marcan "My God, my God" statement, or (see below) his statement that Jesus carried his own cross.

own cross: βαστάζων . . . ἑαυτῷ τὸν σταυρόν. In Lk. 14. 27 Jesus says "Whoever does not take up his cross (ὅστις οὐ βαστάζει τὸν σταυρὸν ἑαυτοῦ) and come after me cannot be my disciple." There can be no question of John here drawing on a tradition which might or might not be related to a Lucan one, for he is here on his own initiative correcting the synoptic tradition to produce a picture of Jesus who, strong and unshaken in his relationship to his Father, was able to carry his own cross. [1] Moreover, it is unlikely that John, in constructing 19. 17, was influenced by Luke's terminology in 14. 27, i.e. in an earlier portion of Luke's gospel—all the moreso as he brings no parallel to Lk. 14. 27 in his gospel.

We have, then, analyzed all the agreements between the Lucan and Johannine pericopes of the crucifixion, death and burial, and have seen that, where the agreements are not coincidental, as in the case of the occurrence of the word εἱστήκεισαν in regard to the women and the absence of a mocking reference to the temple, they are due to John's taking up Lucan elements into his account.

[1] So correctly Windisch, *op. cit.*, pp. 85 f., and Barrett, *op. cit.*, *ad loc.* It may be that John's motive was also to combat a Docetist heresy similar to that later mentioned by Irenaeus, *adv. Haer.* I, XIV, 2, according to which Simon was executed instead of the impassible Jesus. It is true that the usual custom was for a criminal to carry his own cross (see the citations in Bauer, *op. cit.*, *ad loc.*), and that this can be seen as an argument for the historicity of John's account here, hence for its not having originated with John. But this fact does not carry much weight in comparison with the note in Mk. 15. 21 that Simon was the father of Alexander and Rufus, which is the surest of guarantees for the historicity of the Simon tradition.

CHAPTER TWELVE

THE RESURRECTION AND POST-RESURRECTION NARRATIVES

Luke, ch. 24 / John, chs. 20 f.

The Lucan and Johannine accounts of the finding of the empty tomb and the appearance of the risen Christ have the following elements in common: (a) Mary Magdalene (and, in Luke, the women accompanying her) seeks out the tomb before sunrise (Lk. 24. 1, Jn. 20. 1) [1]; (b) two angels [2] appear at the tomb to Mary Magdalene (and the women with her in Luke) (Lk. 24. 2, Jn. 20. 12); (c) several disciples go to the grave on the basis of what Mary Magdalene (in Luke: she and the other women) tells them about its being empty, and find that what they have been told is true (Lk. 24. 24, Jn. 20. 3-10); [3] (d) late on Easter Sunday Jesus appears (Lk. 24. 36: αὐτὸς ἔστη ἐν μέσῳ αὐτῶν; Jn. 20. 19: Ἰησοῦς . . .

[1] John says that it was still dark; Luke uses the phrase ὄρθρου βάθεως which (according to Lidell and Scott, *op. cit.*) means "in the dim morning twilight."

[2] That the two ἄνδρες in Luke are angels is indicated by 24. 23.

[3] A closer Lucan parallel to Jn. 20. 3-10 is Lk. 24. 12. This verse contains a summary of 20. 3-10 (except for the absence of the beloved disciple), with striking verbal similarities; Luke brings among others the following words: μνημεῖον, ἔδραμεν, παρακύψας βλέπει τὰ ὀθόνια μόνα, ἀπῆλθεν πρὸς αὐτόν, John brings μνημεῖον, ἔτρεχον, παρακύψας, βλέπει κείμενα τὰ ὀθόνια, ἀπῆλθον οὖν πάλιν πρὸς αὐτοὺς οἱ μαθηταί. But Lk. 24. 12 is not read by D it Marcion; further, the common vocabulary is predominantly Johannine: ὀθόνια is found elsewhere in the New Testament only in Jn. 19. 40 in the burial account, whereas Luke there has σινδών; ἀπέρχεσθαι πρός occurs three other times in John, never in Luke-Acts; παρακύπτειν is found elsewhere in John (e. g. 20. 11), but never in Luke-Acts. To be sure, some of the phraseology special to Lk. 24. 12 is Lucan: τὸ γεγονός occurs six other times in Luke (and Acts), never in the other three gospels, and ἀνίστημι in participial form preceding the main verb is characteristically Lucan. Hoskyns (*op. cit., ad loc.,*) indeed, maintains that Lk. 24. 12 constitutes an original part of the gospel, and that Lk. 24. 24 is based on it; but the fact that several men are mentioned in v. 24, whereas only Peter is in v. 12, militates against this. On the whole the evidence points to interpolation in v. 12 on the basis of John's account; a scribe who thought that the reference to the disciples' having gone to the tomb in 24. 24 required a mention of the event when it occurred used for this purpose a synopsis from memory of an incident from John—thereby incidentally softening the harsh picture of disbelief given in Lk. 24. 11.

ἔστη εἰς τὸ μέσον) among a group of disciples in Jerusalem, [1] demonstrates his corporeality by showing them his wounds; in connection with both appearances the disciples' joy is mentioned, and Jesus both times speaks to them of the forgiveness of sins and the Spirit, and of the rôle of his hearers—indeed in both cases his words constitute his commission to his Church (Lk. 24. 36-49, Jn. 20. 19-23); [2] (e) both record an appearance of Christ to Peter (Lk. 24. 34, Jn. 21. 1 ff.).

The differences between Luke and John are very many; Luke records that Mary Magdalene, Joanna, Mary (the mother) of James and other women go to the tomb, receive a message of reproof and reminder from the angels, and, recounting what has happened to the disciples, are greeted with disbelief. Then follows Christ's appearance to the two disciples on the way to Emmaus, the return of these two to Jerusalem and to the news that Christ in the meantime has appeared to Peter, the appearance to the eleven and "those with them" and the two Emmaus disciples in Jerusalem, and Christ's ascension from Bethany. [3] In John Mary Magdalene alone comes to the grave and sees the stone pushed aside but no angels; she then fetches Peter and the beloved disciple, who come

[1] That John understands the scene 20. 19-23 as occurring in Jerusalem is clear from the fact that according to him the disciples did not abandon Jesus and flee Jerusalem either at the time of his arrest or later.

[2] Schmid, *Das Evangelium nach Lukas*, *ad loc.*, maintains that Jesus' words, i. e. Lk. 24. 44-49, do not belong together with 24. 36-43 as part of the same scene, but there is no support whatever for this position, which is manifestly motivated by a desire to harmonize the Lucan ascension chronology with that of Acts.

"Peace to you" cannot be counted as an element common to Luke and John, because the B A sah cop sy[sc] reading in Lk. 24. 36 of καὶ λέγει, αὐτοῖς· εἰρήνη ὑμῖν is a gloss from Jn. 20. 19, 26, as the critics (with the exception of von Soden) are agreed. Further, the same group of mss. (with the exception of sy[sc]) offer as v. 40 καὶ τοῦτο εἰπὼν ἔδειξεν (ἐπέδειξεν) αὐτοῖς τὰς χεῖρας καὶ τοὺς ποδάς. This is all but absolutely identical with Jn. 20. 20a, the only significant difference being ποδάς instead of πλευράν; further, the phrase in v. 40 is repetitious after v. 39a (as Jn. 20. 20a, where there's no equivalent of Lk. 24. 39 a, is not); and the critics (again, with von Soden's exception) agree that it is a gloss from John, adapted to Luke by a scribe who substituted "feet" for "side." A further instance of the influence of the Johannine text on Luke at this point is cited by Klostermann (*op. cit.*, *ad loc.*,) in connection with the secondary reading (adduced by G W c f vg sy[p]) in 24. 36 of ἐγώ εἰμι, μὴ φοβεῖσθαι, which he sees as originating in Jn. 6. 20. This is conceivable, but by no means a necessary postulation—for Mk. 6. 50 and the Matthean parallel (Mt. 14. 27) both contain exactly this phrase.

[3] That Luke's gospel closes with the ascension is clear from Acts 1. 2 and the original, long reading of Lk. 24. 51.

to the grave and (in the case of the beloved disciple) to faith, and then return home; whereupon Mary returns, sees the angels, then sees Jesus in the *noli me tangere* scene; Jesus later that day appears to "the disciples" in Jerusalem (it is this scene which is so close to one in Luke), then a week later, also in Jerusalem, to them and to Thomas—and, in the ch. 21 supplement, to Peter and six other disciples by the sea of Galilee. This last—at least vv. 1-14—is in marked contrast to the appearance to Peter as mentioned in Luke which appearance was presumably to Peter alone, and in (or very near) Jerusalem—otherwise the news thereof wouldn't have arrived in Jerusalem by Sunday evening. Furthermore, there are differences in the two accounts of the appearance to the disciples in Jerusalem (Lk. 24. 36-49, Jn. 20. 19-23): in Luke the disciples think they are seeing a ghost, which is the motivation for Jesus' asking for food and eating it—whereupon he reveals the meaning of the scriptures to them, and enjoins them to wait in Jerusalem for the Spirit; in John Jesus' showing of his wounds is not explicitly motivated, and it is followed by the imparting of the Spirit and of the power to forgive or retain sins.

In order to explain where the common material originates, we shall examine in succession the relevant Lucan and Johannine pericopes. Luke's only source in the account of the empty grave is Mark, [1] as 24. 2 (λίθον ἀποκεκυλισμένον cf. Mk. 16. 4) and the transformation in 24. 6 of the Mk. 16. 7 reference to Galilee indicate. [2] His departures from Mark are due to his editorial revising, not to another source: he locates the women's going to the tomb before sunrise in order to stress their zeal, and the mention of not one but two angels appearing at the tomb (24. 4) [3] is to be explained on the basis of Luke's fondness for pairs. [4] Luke doesn't reflect Mark after 16. 7, [5] but goes on to recount two

[1] So correctly Bultmann, *Die Geschichte der synoptischen Tradition*, supplement to p. 310, and Grass, *Ostergeschehen und Osterberichte*, pp. 32-35.

[2] οὐκ ἔστιν ὧδε, ἀλλὰ ἠγέρθη in 24. 6 (cf. Mk. 16. 6) may not in this regard be cited, as these words may not be original—i. e. they're omitted by D it.

[3] That the νεανίσκος in Mark is an angel is clear from his white garment.

[4] e.g. Acts 1. 10. See further the list of pairs in Morgenthaler, *op. cit.*, II, pp. 98, 181. That the notice in 24. 4 stems from the evangelist is indicated further by the fact that ἔσθης (a word appearing in the New Testament only in Luke-Acts—twice—and in James—three times) occurs in it. The vocabulary of vv. 4-5a is, indeed, specifically Lucan: i. e. καὶ ἐγένετο ἐν τῷ . . . καὶ ἰδού, ἐφιστάναι, ἐμφόβων.

[5] Mk. 16. 9-20 is universally acknowledged as a later addition to Mark's gospel, an addition which in 13 reflects Lk. 24. 11.

different resurrection appearances and the ascension from Bethany.

In connection with the first resurrection appearance, the Emmaus story, the question arises how much of it was comprised in the account which Luke took over, and how much he added. [1] Schubert [2] maintains that everything but vv. 13, 15b, 16 and 28-31 stems from Luke, but against this speaks the fact that the disciples' going to the tomb in 24 conflicts with their reaction of disbelief in v. 11, which latter verse definitely stems from Luke and represents his alteration of Mk. 16. 8 in order to make room for the Emmaus story. (To be sure, Luke could have avoided the conflict by constructing v. 11 without mention of scepticism on the part of the disciples; however, that would have resulted in v. 11's being in too flagrant conflict with Mk. 16. 8). The conclusion to be drawn from this is that the Emmaus story was in written form when Luke encountered it, and that the v. 24 tradition of the disciples' going to the tomb was already embedded in it. As for the statement of the eleven in v. 34 that Christ had risen and appeared to Peter, it is incompatible with the reaction of the eleven in v. 37; [3] either Luke inserted v. 34 into a context where 36 ff. already followed on the Emmaus story, or the v. 34 statement (not yet uttered by the eleven) already formed the conclusion of the Emmaus story when Luke took it over, and (putting that statement in the mouths of the eleven) he joined the account of the appearance to the eleven on to it, despite the resulting unevenness. In view of the fact that the individual pericopes of Luke's resurrection and post-resurrection narrative were in every other instance joined together by Luke (who connected the Emmaus story to the account of the empty tomb, and—see nt. 21—the ascension account to that of the appearance to the eleven in Jerusalem), and that they all fit together into an Easter day scheme [4] which in its very patness

[1] Even the most radical critics are agreed that the story at least in its rudiments did not originate with Luke.

[2] Paul Schubert, 'The Structure and Significance of Luke 24' in *Neutestamentliche Studien für Rudolf Bultmann*, p. 174.

[3] D Origen's reading of λέγοντες in 24. 34, which makes the Emmaus disciples the speakers, is surely secondary: where would the Emmaus disciples have heard of such an appearance? To assume that they are referring to their own experience by means of the conjecture that the second disciple was named Simon is totally unjustified—such a case would require the reading ἡμῖν, not Σίμωνι, in v. 34.

[4] Rengstorf, *op. cit.*, *ad loc.*, maintains that Luke in ch. 24 doesn't intend to convey that the ascension occurred on Easter Sunday, but he offers no evidence to support this assertion, and indeed none exists.

appears artificial, originating in all likelihood with Luke[1]—in view of these things the second of these alternatives is the more likely. The v. 34 tradition, then, was found by Luke imbedded in the Emmaus story, and it referred to a resurrection appearance of Christ, his first, [2] occurring in or near Jerusalem.

As for the account of the appearance to the disciples in Jerusalem, the fact that Jesus eats the fish but the disciples do not, i.e. that it does not fulfil the qualifications mentioned in Acts 10. 41 (where Peter defines the witnesses to the resurrection as those who had eaten and drunk with the resurrected Christ) [3] shows that Luke, in taking over the story, altered the details of what must already have been a written account very little. That he transferred the locale of the story from the sea of Galilee to Jerusalem has been suspected [4] on the basis of the fact that fish belong in the former but not the latter milieu—in which case the account would be somewhat closer to Jn. 21. 1 ff. But fish were available in Jerusalem,

[1] The clearest indication of this artificiality is that Luke himself departs from the scheme in Acts 1, where, in the tradition of a longer period of time for the resurrection appearances, he will have been following a tradition which existed before him.

[2] It is possible that the appearance to the Emmaus disciples preceded it, but news of Peter's encounter reached Jerusalem first, and it would therefore count as the first.

[3] That is to say, the eating is here a proof of Jesus' physical resurrection; as such it concerns those present, but it does not qualify them as witnesses who participated in a meal with Jesus (The fact that only Jesus eats shows further that the eating has no sacramental or symbolic significance. It was incorrectly understood to have such significance by the scribe who later inserted καὶ ἀπὸ μελίσσιου κηρίον, after v. 43—honey being given to the newly-baptized in Tertullian's time, as Tertullian, *De corona militis* 3, *Adversus Marcionem* I, 14, reports.) Doubtless the secondary readings of 24. 43 offered by θ vg φ sy[c], according to which Jesus gives fish to the disciples to eat, represent the influence of Jn. 21. 13 (where the disciples do eat) on the Lucan text. It is, however, not legitimate to regard the whole incident of Jesus' eating the fish in the Lucan passage as a gloss, as Grant, *op. cit.*, p. 301, does. A further similarity between the original text of Lk. 24. 36-49 and Jn. 21. 1 ff. exists in that both record Jesus as asking the question "Have you something to eat?" (Lk. 24. 41, Jn. 21. 5), though the two statements are not similar in Greek beyond the fact that both contain the word ἔχετε. We saw above (p. 13) that John utilized a written source in 21. 1-14; we may therefore assume that Jesus' question in 21. 5 does not stem from him (in which case he would here be echoing Luke), but was part of the account when it came to him. In all likelihood, however, the occurrence of the similar questions points to a connection between the two stories at an earlier stage in their transmission.

[4] By Bultmann, *op. cit.*, p. 310, and by Creed and Klostermann in their commentaries, *ad loc.*

as Nehemiah 13. 16, 23. 16 shows, and to conclude that the story belongs on the sea of Galilee on the basis of the fact that fish were more easily available there is to read too much into the text. [1] The location of the appearance on Sunday afternoon, however, is part of the Lk. 24 Sunday scheme; in all likelihood, therefore, it stems from Luke. [2]

John in his account of the empty tomb is substantially independent of the synoptic gospels. [3] There are two elements in his account, (a) that of Mary Magdalene alone at the grave encountering the angels and then Jesus, and (b) Peter's and the beloved disciple's running to the grave and finding it empty. That John combined the two is clear from the ways in which they do not mesh: (a) Mary's stooping down and looking into the tomb is first mentioned in 20. 11, although her words in 20. 2 presuppose such action on her part; (b) Mary doesn't, inexplicably, meet the two disciples as she is returning to the tomb and they are coming from it; (c) the two disciples, unlike Mary, do not see the two angels at the tomb, though Mary has seen them there only a short time before. The usual explanation for this unevenness is that John created the incident of the two disciples, and wove it into the Mary Magdalene episode. [4] Support for this view is seen in the fact that the incident

[1] So correctly Grass, *op. cit.*, p. 40.

[2] Unlike the first seven verses of the passage, the discourse which comprises the concluding six verses stems from the evangelist, as a comparison of the material and vocabulary with that elsewhere in the gospel shows: vv. 44b-45 cf. v. 27, 4. 81-21; v. 46 a cf. v. 26 a; v. 47 a cf. Acts 17. 30, 2. 38; v. 47 b cf. Acts. 1. 8; v. 47 b ἀρξάμενοι ἀπό cf. 23. 5, Acts 10. 37; v. 48 μάρτυρες cf. Acts 1. 8, 22, 2. 32, 3. 15 etc. As for the departure of Christ from Bethany, though the location stems from oral tradition (as Luke's failure to show any interest in Bethany elsewhere shows), the mirroring of the ascension stems from Luke (e.g. v. 52 represents the carrying out of the v. 49 b command, preparatory to Acts. 1 f.; v. 53 cf. Acts. 2. 46), and is joined by him on to the preceding appearance account in order to provide a fitting conclusion to the Easter Sunday scheme and to the gospel. It conflicts, to be sure, with Acts. 1. 3, 9; but on the basis of this to postulate that 24. 50-53 and Acts. 1. 1-5 are secondary, as Lake, *The Beginnings of Christianity*, vol. 5, pp. 3 f., and following him Menoud, "Remarques sur les textes de l'ascension dans Luc-Actes," pp. 148-157, *Neutestamentliche Studien für Rudolf Bultmann*, do, is unwarranted; the conflicts arises from Luke's having written two books, the second of which he wished to have begin with the ascension—but the first of which he felt could end with nothing else.

[3] Though John in 20. 1, like Lk. 24. 1, reads τῇ δὲ μιᾷ τῶν σαββάτων, dependence on Luke here cannot, despite Larfeld, *op. cit.*, p. 354, be postulated, because Mk. 16. 2 reads τῇ μιᾷ τῶν σαββάτων.

[4] So Bultmann, *Das Evangelium des Johannes, ad loc.*, Dibelius, *Zeitschrift für die Alttestamentliche Wissenschaft*, supplement 33, p. 136.

of Peter and the beloved disciple redounds, as always when the two men are juxtaposed, to the credit of the latter: the beloved disciple runs faster, gets to the tomb first, looks in and sees its emptiness first, and believes (i.e. in the resurrection) first. But this scheme is significantly broken at one point: Peter enters the tomb first. The degree of incongruity arising therefrom is clear from the contrast between two statements both made about the beloved disciple: v. 4 ἦλθεν εἰς τὸ μνημεῖον and v. 5 οὐ μέντοι εἰσῆλθεν. The only adequate explanation is that John is here revising a tradition according to which Peter coming to the tomb was the first of the disciples to enter it—whereupon, presumably, he came to faith. [1] We cannot be absolutely sure whether the tradition as John found it already spoke of a second disciple (perhaps John the son of Zebedee) accompanying Peter. But one sign that it did is the fact that Lk. 24. 24 mentions more than one disciple as going to the grave; for Lk. 24. 24 constitutes, in fact, a variant of the tradition which John in 20. 3-10 utilized. [2] There are disparities between the two forms of this tradition as we have it, e.g. "him they did not see" in Luke in contrast to the mention of belief in John; however, what is different is not significant enough in comparison with what is similar to justify regarding what we find as two different traditions rather than two different forms of the same one [3] We

[1] John does not explicitly say in the present passage that Peter believed, though he does say that the beloved disciple did. Bultmann, *op. cit.*, *ad loc.*, and Grass, *op. cit.*, p. 56, say that John has not suppressed Peter's belief, but meant to convey that Peter like the beloved disciple believed; Bultmann even thinks that the evangelist implies that Peter believed in vv. 6 f., before the beloved disciple. But Peter's action in vv. 6 f. is no different from that of the beloved disciple in v. 5, and it's nevertheless not said that the latter believed until v. 8. Surely John's silence as regards Peter in contrast to the other disciple is significant; John doesn't explicitly contradict the previous tradition that Peter believed at the grave—he is, as it were, purposely vague on the subject. It is this failure to be specific which characterizes John's treatment of Peter at this point—a treatment which results in the neutralization of Peter's position, in contrast to that of the beloved disciple. An indication of the validity of this explanation is to be found in Lk. 24. 12, where the glossator echoing the Johannine passage didn't record Peter's belief, but only his astonishment—the former is not to be read out of Jn. 20. 6. (It is far-fetched when Grass, *op. cit.*, p. 34, maintains that the glossator of 24. 12 purposely recorded not Peter's belief but his astonishment, despite the mention of the former in the Johannine text, in order to make 24. 12 conform to Lk. 24. 24).

[2] So correctly Schniewind, *op. cit.*, p. 88. On Lk. 24. 24 see above, p. 88.

[3] So correctly Gardner-Smith, *op. cit.*, p. 77. The difference, then, between Lk. 24. 24 and 24. 12 in relation to Jn. 20. 3-10 is that the former is indepen-

shall have more to say about the relationship between its form in Luke and its form in John when we discuss its historicity below.

John in combining the two elements in 20. 1-18 has at two points drawn on Luke, i.e. as regards the placing of Mary's visit before sunrise, and as regards the appearance of two angels at the tomb. [1] The first he drew on because, like Luke, he wished to stress Mary's zeal. The second he drew on for the sake of conformity to the prevailing (Lucan) tradition, drawing all the details of the angels' appearance from the preceding and following verses of his gospel: the only function of the angels is to ask a question which Jesus, when he appears, repeats—a question which, when the angels ask it, Mary answers with the same words she used with the disciples in v. 2; it is clear from this that the 20. 11-18 scene in its pre-Johannine form began only with the appearance of Jesus to Mary. [2]

As for the 20. 19-23 resurrection appearance, in view of the fact that John knew Luke's gospel, the similarity to Lk. 24. 36-43 is too great to be accidental. Luke is, in fact, John's source here. [3] He derived from him Jesus' sudden appearance "in the midst" of the disciples, [4] the timing of the appearance on Sunday afternoon,

---

dent of the present Johannine text (though not of the tradition lying behind it), whereas the latter is not.

[1] Wellhausen, *Das Evangelium Johannis, ad loc.*, maintains that Jn. 20. 12 f. is a gloss, but, lacking manuscript evidence to the contrary, it is better to see the evangelist rather than a later hand as here conforming his account to the Lucan version.

[2] Schniewind, who maintains that John did not know Luke's gospel, has to admit (*op. cit.*, p. 86) that John must have known of a tradition of the angel's appearance similar to that which is found in Luke. Not a similar tradition, but Luke itself!

[3] This is to be emphasized in opposition to Bultmann, *op. cit., ad loc.*, who here as always overlooks Luke's role as a source for John, and attributes Jn. 20. 19-23, as well as the following pericope, to the running source which he postulates for John. Loisy, *l'Evangile selon Luc*, does not see John as here dependent on Luke, but rather as drawing on John. This position is dependent on his view that John is an earlier gospel than Luke, and hence was not known to the third evangelist; but, as the anointing pericopes once and for all show, this view of the chronology of the gospels is not justified by the evidence of their contents. Grant, *op. cit.*, p. 301, regards Lk. 24. 37, 39-43 as a gloss derived almost exclusively from Jn. 20 f. material, but this view, which lacks manuscripts support, is surely less convincing than that holding that the similarities are due to John's drawing on Luke.

[4] John does not bring ἐν μέσῳ but the *koine* form εἰς τὸ μέσον—cf. Mk. 3. 3. John's note that the doors were locked merely represents, as Klostermann, *op. cit., ad loc.*, has seen, his effort to make clear the miraculous content which is already implicit in Lk. 24. 31. Goguel, *Zeitschrift für die Neutestamentliche Wissenschaft* 1932, p. 291 and Bultmann, *op. cit., ad loc.*, maintain

its location in Jerusalem and the emphasis on the physical nature of Jesus' body. [1] To be sure, the original nature of the appearance as recounted by Luke, in which the disciples' unbelief (to which their joy in v. 41 is subordinate) is overcome by proofs of increasing power, is no longer clear. John has recast the account. The proof of his physicality now occurs on Jesus' initiative, [2] and is conformed to the Johannine account according to which Jesus' side was pierced. The group to whom Jesus appears is no longer the eleven and "those with them" and the two Emmaus disciples, but "the disciples" (v. 19), a group whose size it is here as elsewhere in John's gospel impossible to determine, and who, as vv. 21-23 show, are meant to represent the Church. The joy of the disciples is now associated with their belief not their unbelief, and is therefore no longer ambiguous. [3] For Jesus' words John does not draw on Luke but primarily on his own Spirit-given knowledge: εἰρήνη ὑμῖν 19b cf. 21a, 26b; [4] 21b cf. 17.18. Jesus' statements include one non-Johannine element, the conferring on the disciples of the power to forgive and retain sins in v. 23; [5] Luke at the corresponding point also mentions forgiveness of sins, though in an

---

there is no historical basis for any fear of persecution of the disciples' part, but that is not John's view, as 7. 13 and 19. 38. show.

[1] The theme of touching Jesus, which appears in Luke, does not appear here, but in the following passage, vv. 24-29. The fact that ψηλαφᾶν, which appears in Luke (24. 39) and significantly in 1 Jn. 1. 1, does not appear in Jn. 20. 24-29, constitutes an argument against the gospel's and the first epistle's having the same author.

[2] John's account is here clearly secondary as over against Luke's—a fact which constitutes a problem for Bultmann, *op. cit.*, *ad loc.*, who admits that something similar to Lk. 24. 37 f. must have been a part of John's source. Not something similar, but Lk. 24. 37 f. itself! Wellhausen, *op. cit.*, *ad loc.*, and following him Zurhellen, *op. cit.*, p. 45, conclude from what they term the lack of motivation for Jesus' showing his wounds to the disciples in 20. 20 that this verse is a gloss. But both critics also maintain that Lk. 24. 40 is a gloss, a gloss which it is universally acknowledged originates in Jn. 20. 20. As it is exceedingly unlikely that one gloss served as the basis for another, we conclude that Jn. 20. 20 is part of the original text.

[3] Grass, *op. cit.*, p. 40, weighs the possibility that the mention of joy in Lk. 24. 41 may be a gloss deriving from Jn. 20. 20 b. There is, however, as he himself acknowledges, no manuscript support for this; and the phrase ἀπὸ τῆς χαρᾶς in 24. 41 is Lucan—cf. Acts 12. 14, Lk. 22. 45.

[4] Considering its three-fold repetition this phrase may not be understood to constitute a mere conventional form but is rather an extension of 14. 27.

[5] That this is not a characteristically Johannine element is clear from its contrast with the material of ch. 13-17, and with the lack of mention of forgiveness of sins anywhere else in the gospel; John is here clearly conforming his account to prevailing Church tradition.

entirely differing immediate context; despite this latter fact it is likely that Luke's mention of the subject caused John to insert at this point a piece of (possibly oral) tradition circulating in the Church and dealing with the same subject. John departs from Luke markedly in that the Spirit (which he calls the Holy Spirit) is not promised but is given. [1] To consider this as primarily a correction of Luke on John's part is to misjudge John's intent; even if John knew Acts and its account of the giving of the Spirit which is in conflict with his own, his interest here was not primarily chronological, and therefore his intention was not to correct Luke. He saw in the giving of the Holy Spirit the fulfilment of 7. 39a. There being for him, as for Matthew and Mark, no room for a second book following on the gospel he was writing, it was natural that the fulfilment of 7. 39a would occur within the compass of that gospel. There is no question, however, but that his account *does* conflict with Luke's. [2] But his debt to Luke is also clear; Luke's mention of the Spirit, though not of its imparting, probably caused John to locate the imparting of the Spirit (and the commission to the Church which accompanies it, though as Mt. 28. 16-20 shows, that belongs anyway to the end of a gospel) at the corresponding point in his gospel.

John's debt to Luke in 20. 19-23 is, then, clear. The extent to which he is in debt to Luke in 20. 24-29 is not so clear. Certainly the detail that Christ stood in the midst of the disciples in v. 26, like the corresponding note in v. 19, stems from Lk. 24. 36; so too the location of the appearance on a Sunday stems from Luke. Whether one thinks that the other element which Jn. 20. 24-29 has in common with 19-23, i.e. the location in Jerusalem, also originated in Lk. 24. 36-43, depends on whether one thinks the

[1] In view of Jesus' statement to Mary Magdalene in 20. 17 a, it is clear from Jesus' command to Thomas in 20. 27 that John regards Jesus as having in the meantime ascended to the Father. Because Jesus, though he shows the disciples his wounds in 20. 19-23, does not there bid them touch him, it is probable that John regards Jesus' ascension as occurring (at the close of Easter Sunday?) between this appearance and the one a week later. According to John, the imparting of the Holy Spirit precedes the ascension, whereas in Luke-Acts the order is reversed. What further separates John from Luke is the lack of description of the ascension in his gospel—in marked contrast to Lk. 24. 51, Acts 1. 9.

[2] Hoskyns, *op. cit., ad loc.*, maintains that John recounts a giving of the Spirit which, as Christ has not yet ascended, is preliminary, and subordinate, to the definitive giving as recounted in Acts; but this is illegitimate harmonization.

20. 24-29 incident originated with John or already existed before him in written or oral form. In the former case the element of touching originated in Lk. 24. 39, the rôle of Thomas originated with John (who mentions him seven other times in the course of the gospel), and the note that he was one of the twelve likewise stems from John, who thus introduces a subtle polemic against the twelve in contrast to those who believe without seeing (v. 29). The last element of this hypothesis is an attractive one, conforming well to John's diminution of the rôle of the twelve elsewhere in his gospel. But the view that the doubting Thomas incident originated in John's mind is, nevertheless, quite possibly unduly sceptical; it is part of a complex of traditions about Thomas which John brings, but which there is no compelling reason to think he invented. Actually, certainty as to the source of 20. 24-29 is not possible; all we can say is that either John knew another tradition strikingly parallel to Lk. 24. 36-49 (for if Thomas's name was part of it, so also were the details about the touching and the place), or he was so impressed by the Lucan passage that he used it as the basis of not one but two parallel incidents in his gospel.

As for the resurrection appearance to Peter in Jn. 21, the passage 21. 1-23 consists of three units, vv. 1-14, vv. 15-18 and vv. 20-23, which had no connection with each other until John (who, on the basis of the v. 22 statement, composed the third) put them together. [1] The first two are both parallel to Lk. 24. 34 in that both recount an appearance to Peter; the second is closer than the first to Lk. 24. 34 in that it involves an appearance to Peter alone, and in that it probably was not connected to Galilee till John joined it to 21. 1-14. There can, however, be no question of John's having drawn on Lk. 24. 34 as a source for 20. 15-19; for 24. 34 is of too fragmentary a nature to have provided any of the material for the latter.

We have therewith completed the analysis of the literary relationships between Luke's and John's accounts of the finding of the empty tomb and the resurrection appearances, and conclude that John in 20.12 and in 20. 19-29 made use of Lucan material—though of how much in 25-29 is not clear—but that the similarity between Lk. 24. 23 f. and Jn. 20. 2-10 cannot be so explained, the evidence pointing rather to a common tradition at the root of

---

[1] On Jn. 21. 15-19 see p. 41 and nt. 3 there.

both passages. As for the references in both gospels to the appearance to Peter, there is no evidence of literary connection between them, though they point to the same event.

One question remains unanswered, that of the historicity of the common material as regards the resurrection appearances. [1] As for the tradition that two disciples went to Jesus' grave and found it empty, it is very likely historical. [2] It is not surprising that two disciples went to see for themselves on the basis of what the women told them. [3] To be sure, in Luke this conflicts with 24. 11, but as we saw the conflict is due to the fact that in 24. 24 Luke is taking up older tradition, whereas in 24. 11 he is altering Mark so as to minimize the conflict between the Marcan tradition and that embodied in the Emmaus story. Lk. 24. 24 also conflicts with Mk. 16. 8, where the women, fearful, do not even tell the disciples what they have experienced; but this motif of fear is typically Marcan, [4] and is used by him to break off his gospel after the angel has reminded the women that Galilee is the place where Jesus will appear—at the parousia. [5] A further argument against the Lk. 24. 24 tradition, advanced on the basis of Mk. 14. 27-50, is that all the disciples except the women left Jerusalem at the time

[1] The detail of the women going to the tomb before sunrise, and the detail of the two angels (instead of one) at the tomb, originate, as we saw, with the evangelist Luke.

[2] The presupposition of this statement is that the tradition of the empty grave is an historical one. It is not our purpose here to discuss this question, because the empty grave tradition is shared not only by Luke and John but by the other two evangelists as well; we shall rather discuss the issues raised by the part of that tradition involving the two disciples. Those critics who reject the tradition as a whole will of course reject this particular part of it.

[3] Gardner-Smith, *op. cit.*, p. 76, sees Lk. 24. 24 as arising out of an attempt to provide better evidence (i. e. the witness of men and not women) for the empty tomb than had previously existed, but this is unduly sceptical.

[4] Cf. Mk. 4. 41, 9. 6, 10. 32; Matthew cancels the mention of fear at all three points, Luke at the second and third.

[5] So correctly Lohmeyer, *Das Evangelium des Markus, ad loc.*, and *Galiläa und Jerusalem*, p. 12, and following him Marxsen, *op. cit.*, pp. 75 ff. (Lohmeyer's view is correct, despite the fact that the terminological distinction on which he based it—according to which ὁρᾶν in the passive voice refers to resurrection appearances, and ὁρᾶν in the active voice to the parousia—is not correct, as 1 Cor. 9. 1 and Jn. 20. 16, 25, 29 show.) This interpretation presupposes a background of confusion and dispute about the meaning of the resurrection appearances as such, as well as about where they occurred (this last was also asserted by Harnack, *The Acts of the Apostles*, pp. 156 f.), which gave rise to Mark's effort to provide a solution not by pointing to events of the past, but to an impending event, that of the parousia. Mk. 16. 8 constitutes, then, the original ending of the gospel.

of the arrest, and so could not possibly have visited the tomb; but this is not said by Mark, and, indeed, Mk. 16. 7 presupposes the disciples' presence in Jerusalem.[1] The tradition in its basic, Lucan form appears, then, to be sound; the same cannot however, be said for the Johannine form of the tradition. For it is unlikely that belief in the resurrection originated in the experience of the empty tomb rather than in that of the resurrection appearances;[2] John's version of the discovery of the empty tomb is in this regard secondary to that of the other three evangelists. John's account of the faith of the beloved disciple goes back, as we saw, to an account of Peter's coming to faith; the latter account arose, we may assume, out of a crossing of the tradition of two disciples going to the tomb (where, however, neither came to faith as the result of finding it empty) with that of the appearance of the resurrected Jesus to Peter mentioned by Paul and Luke. One element special to the Johannine tradition may, however, belong to the original tradition of which we have merely the bare outlines in Luke, i.e. that according to which the two disciples involved were Peter and John.[3]

We come now to the tradition of the appearance to Peter. That Christ did appear to Peter, and that it constituted his first resurrection appearance, is universally acknowledged.[4] The question here to be asked is, where did the appearance occur—in or near Jerusalem (as Lk. 24. 34 reports) or in Galilee (as John's source in Jn. 21. 1-14 recounted)? This question is bound up with that of where Christ appeared to the eleven, for it is generally agreed that where Christ appeared to Peter he also, soon after, appeared to the eleven.

The prevailing German critical view[5] denies the historicity of the Jerusalem appearance to Peter and the eleven, and speaks instead of the flight of the eleven to Galilee, the appearance of

[1] It is clear from 16. 7 that Mark regards 14. 50 as referring to a flight of the disciples from Jesus' side, but not from Jerusalem.

[2] So correctly Grass, *op. cit.*, p. 56, who opposes von Campenhausen, *Der Ablauf der Osterereignisse und das leere Grab*, p. 46. This issue is quite a different one than that of whether the tomb was empty or not.

[3] The question may be asked why Luke was content to record this incident in such a sketchy fashion. The answer is that, since the disciples did not come to faith as a result of it, he did not regard it as important.

[4] So, for example, Cullmann, *Peter*, p. 63.

[5] Grass, *op. cit.*, pp. 121 f., cites in this regard Dobschütz, Harnack, Holl, Hirsch, von Campenhausen and the "whole liberal school of critics" (e. g. Bultmann). Among the French Goguel, *La Foi à la Resurrection de Jésus dans le Christianisme Primitif*, pp. 310-15, may be cited.

Jesus to Peter and then to all the eleven there, and their subsequent return to Jerusalem; the tradition of the first appearances as occurring in Jerusalem was, according to this view, later invented in the interests of the Church in Jerusalem. This position finds its support in the following passages: (a) Mk. 14. 27, 49, which, it is maintained, refer to the coming flight of the disciples to Galilee; (b) the (postulated) original ending of Mark which is supposed to have recounted one or several appearances in Galilee; (c) the ending of Matthew, seen as echoing the original, Galilean resurrection appearance tradition; (d) the ending of Peter's gospel at a point where an initial appearance to Peter and several other disciples in Galilee is about to be narrated; (e) the appearance recounted in Jn. 21. 1-14.

We shall examine each of these passages in turn. In the first place, neither Mk. 14. 27 nor 14. 49 speaks of Galilee; no doubt Jesus at the end was abandoned by the eleven—there is no other explanation for their failure to ask for his body and bury it—but as was said above there is no mention, either in Mark or Matthew, of flight to Galilee. As for the original, Galilean ending of Mark, it is, as we saw, a myth. [1] As for Matthew, 28. 16-20 is located in Galilee, but that does not so much recount a resurrection appearance as Jesus' parting words with a setting provided by Matthew for them, i.e. a location on a mountain parallel to that of the chs. 5-7 sermon and the transfiguration, and in Galilee because (as 28. 10 shows) of Matthew's misunderstanding of Mk. 16. 7 as referring to a resurrection appearance not the parousia. Matthew neither here nor elsewhere in the passion and resurrection account had a reliable source other than Mark. [2] Peter's gospel may not be counted as an independent witness, for it is very unlikely that it is in its ending independent of Jn. 21; it has, indeed, never been conclusively demonstrated that at any point its author had a source other than the four canonical gospels; [3] this, joined with

---

[1] See p. 96, nt. 5. That the great majority of scholars, including Creed, Lightfoot, Enslin, Dibelius and Jeremias, hold to the view of the writer is clear from the list of those favoring and opposing it in Bultmann, *Geschichte der synoptischen Tradition*, supplement to p. 309.

[2] This is clear when one lists Matthew's special passion and resurrection material, e.g. Pilate's wife's dream, the guard at the tomb, the unsealing of the grave on Easter morning, the bribing of the soldiers, Christ's appearance (overshadowing that of the angel) to the women near the tomb.

[3] So correctly Burkitt, *Christian Beginnings*, p. 79.

the fact of his frequent use of the fourth gospel, [1] and the attractiveness of Jn. 21 to him because of the important role Peter there plays, points to his use of Jn. 21 at the end of his gospel. [2]

There remains only Jn. 21. 1-14. But Jn. 21. 1-14 recounts neither an appearance to Peter alone nor to the eleven, but rather to seven disciples. The account in its present form can have developed neither from an account of an appearance to Peter alone, nor from a tradition of an appearance to the eleven; furthermore, John's source in 21. 1-14 recorded a first appearance, not one following a previous appearance to Peter alone. Jn. 21. 1-14 conflicts, therefore, not only with the Lucan and Jn. 20 accounts, but also with Paul's account (1 Cor. 15. 4 ff.), a factor generally overlooked by the advocates of the hypothesis.

The latter explain the return of Peter and the other ten to Jerusalem after the appearances in Galilee on the ground that there's where every Jew expected the end to come. [3] But surely any preconceived notion of the end as focussing around Jerusalem would be blotted out by the overwhelming experience of encountering the risen Christ in Galilee! Where he appeared once would be clearly the place where they'd expect him to return; they would stay there, and the Church would logically have its center there, where too Jesus in his lifetime had found the greatest response. But we know from Gal. 1 that at the time of Paul's conversion the Church had its center in Jerusalem, and of a Church in Galilee we hear next to nothing at all.[4] Grass himself[5] locates the appearance to the five hundred which Paul mentions in Jerusalem, by which time the Church was already centered there. In order to explain an immediate removal to Jerusalem following upon appearances in Galilee, it is necessary to postulate that in the course of one of these appearances Christ commanded his disciples to

---

[1] For a list of the points at which Peter draws on John see von Schubert, *Die Composition des Pseudopetrinischen Evangelienfragments*, pp. 159 ff.

[2] So Stülcken, pp. 87 f. in *Handbuch zu den Neutestamentlichen Apokryphen*, ed. E. Hennecke, followed by Finegan, *op. cit.*, p. 100.

[3] Grass, *op. cit.*, p. 117, nt. 2 cites in this regard Strack-Billerback, *op. cit.*, II, p. 300, and Mk. 13. 14-26.

[4] Paul makes no mention of Churches in Galilee; Acts 9. 31 does, but that reference is made problematical by the fact that there is no mention of where in Galilee these were located. The picture one therefore receives is one of a few scattered Christians in Galilee, whose presence there was not due to the preaching of any of the apostles.

[5] Grass, *op. cit.*, p. 122, following Holl.

return to Jerusalem. But we hear nothing of this in any extant tradition, though such a feature would hardly have been suppressed by the Church in Jerusalem which would owe its existence to it.

In view of all these factors it is far more natural to postulate that Christ appeared to Peter near Jerusalem; either Peter was hiding there in discouragement, separated from the other disciples, or he was actually on his way back to Galilee. At any event, the effect of the appearance was to cause him to rejoin, or perhaps to rally, the other ten in Jerusalem, where Christ then appeared to them, and where they subsequently began to preach. [1] This explains the ineradicable identification of the twelve with the city from the beginning, [2] and the totally secondary position of Galilee despite the fact that Jesus lived there until the last few days of his life. The fact that the first appearances occurred in Jerusalem does not mean that none occurred in Galilee; in all likelihood some did, as most of the people who had known Jesus lived in Galilee; it is against a background of appearances in both places, and of conflicting reports about them, that Mark's conclusion to his gospel must be understood, as we saw above. Nevertheless, in view of the agreement on essentials between Paul and Luke, plus what we know of the rôle Jerusalem played in the Church, we may safely affirm that the *first* appearances occurred in Jerusalem, not in Galilee. To be sure, the appearance in Jn. 21. 1-14, which goes back to the account of a first appearance in Galilee, remains problematical; but to assume, despite (or just because of!) the conflict of this account with the witness of the rest of the New Testament, that it must be historical, represents an unbalanced judgment. Indeed, the fourth evangelist himself did not hold to the view of a first appearance in Galilee, as his revision of his source in 21. 1-14 shows—nor did he include an appearance in Galilee in the gospel as he at first wrote it (i.e. chs. 1-20) at all. The best explanation of why he later added the Galilean appearance is that he wished his gospel to include a Galilean appearance as well as Jerusalem ones in order to foster its acceptance by those who, in the controversy over the "where" of the appearances, maintained that the risen Christ had appeared in Galilee. For that reason he

[1] This explanation of the occurrences originates with Burkitt, *op. cit.*, pp. 86 f.

[2] The only exception to this rule was Peter, as Galatians and Acts recount.

located all of ch. 21 in Galilee, including vv. 15-19 (which he tacked on to the appearance to the seven), though as we saw the material in these verses originally had no connection with that in vv. 1-14 and therefore, in all likelihood, none with Galilee; vv. 15-19, indeed, contain along with Lk. 22. 31 f. [1] the only detailed record of what occurred at Christ's appearance to Peter in or near Jerusalem which has come down to us. [2]

If Luke is essentially historical in his representation of the "where" of the first resurrection appearances, the same cannot, as we saw, be said to be true of the "when;" the view that all the appearances occurred on Sunday originates with him. He was clearly a molder of tradition in this regard, for John, in placing the appearance to Thomas a week after that to the other disciples and so locating all Jerusalem appearances on Sunday, follows him. The question of the historicity of Jesus' proving the physicality of his resurrected body by showing his wounds is an unanswerable one, as is the case with the historicity of all the details of what occurred during resurrection appearances. Three points may be made, however, in connection with it: (a) though Mark and following him Matthew do not mention it, Christ in all likelihood *was* nailed by the hands and feet to the cross, as this was the usual procedure in connection with crucifixion; [3] (b) the issue of the physicality of Christ's resurrected body as it arises in this regard can't be separated from the same issue as it occurs in connection with the empty grave; the matter, then, doesn't exist only in two of the four gospels, but in all four, going back to the beginning of the gospel tradition; (c) the Church's interest in combating Docetism was a factor very early (cf. Jn. 1. 14), and may quite likely have given rise to this feature of the resurrection appearances.

[1] On these verses see pp. 41 f. above.

[2] The question may be asked why neither Luke nor John recount more directly Christ's appearance to Peter. If we may judge from Lk. 22. 31 f., the answer may have to do with the fact that Jesus' words of commission to Peter which no doubt formed the core of the appearance referred to the disciples' abandonment of Jesus, an event neither Luke nor John recorded.

[3] So Zöckler, *Das Kreuz Christi*, p. 103, who cites (a) the fact that the nails used for the purpose were proverbial in the Roman world for their hardness and firmness, and (b) the fact that Xenophon of Ephesus cites (*Ephesiaka* 4. 22) the practice among the Egyptians of fastening criminals to the cross merely by ropes, which he would hardly do if this were the custom prevailing everywhere.

We conclude, then that the Lucan account of the running of several disciples to the empty tomb, and of the "where" of the appearances to Peter and the twelve, draws on historically accurate tradition—a verdict supported by John's account both in its agreements with and departures from Luke's account.

CHAPTER THIRTEEN

CONCLUSION: JESUS' ACTIVITY IN SAMARIA AND THE TRADITIONS COMMON TO LUKE AND JOHN

Both Luke and John record that Jesus in the course of his ministry set foot in Samaria and found there a response of faith. Luke recounts that Jesus, intending to enter a Samaritan village at the beginning of his trip to Jerusalem, sent messengers to prepare his way, who were rejected by the villagers (9. 51-56), whereupon Jesus and the disciples went on to "another village;" later on in the course of the journey, touching at least on the borders of Samaritan territory, [1] Jesus heals ten men of leprosy, only one of whom, a Samaritan, thanks him, whereupon he says to the Samaritan "Rise, go, your faith has saved you" (17. 11-19). The fact that Jesus after 9. 56 is mentioned as being in Samaritan territory makes it possible that Luke meant by "another village" [2] another Samaritan village, [3] though certainty on the point is not to be achieved. At any event, Luke's placing 17. 11-19 after 9. 52-56 and not before it is his way of showing that Jesus was not deterred by the reception accorded his messengers in 9. 52-56, and that the last word as regards the Samaritans was not one of rejection but of faith (17. 19). [4] Thus in Luke's gospel we have an anticipation

[1] That much is clear, whatever the difficult phrase διὰ μέσον Σαμαρείας καὶ Γαλιλαίας in 17. 11 may mean. The phrase is problematical in both the construction δία with accusitive μέσον, and the mention of Samaria preceding that of Galilee. As regards the latter, Hirsch's explanation (*Frühgeschichte des Evangeliums*, II, p. 227) that Samaria comes first because that is the way a narrator writing from the point of view of Judea would think of the journey from Galilee to Judea, does not correspond to the facts of experience. Lohse's suggestion ("Missionarisches Handeln Jesu nach dem Evangelium des Lukas," *Theologische Zeitschrift* 1954, pp. 7 f.) that Samaria is mentioned first because the story focuses on a Samaritan is a better one, though the sequence remains puzzling.

[2] What happened there is not recorded.

[3] K. L. Schmidt, *Die Rahmen der Geschichte Jesu*, pp. 267 f., is certain this is the case. Conzelmann, *op. cit.*, p. 53, though he correctly cites the parallel between the rejection in Samaria at the beginning of the journey section and the rejection in Nazareth at the beginning of the Galilean section, is certainly wrong—as 17. 11 shows—in concluding from the parallel that Luke meant to convey that Jesus in 9. 56 once and for all quit Samaria.

[4] This impression is strengthened by Luke's placing of the parable of the good Samaritan in ch. 14.

in Jesus' lifetime of the Church's missionary activity among the Samaritans as it is recorded in Acts 8, an anticipation which serves to justify the latter. Indeed, though the travel narrative 9. 51-18. 14 contains much Galilean material, [1] Luke by placing a Samaritan pericope at the beginning of it has, at the price of creating an obvious geographical discrepancy between that pericope and much of what follows, implicitly associated the whole travel narrative with Samaria, as the previous section is associated with Galilee and the following with Jerusalem. [2] Luke, then, has immensely magnified the importance of the Samaritan material. He has, however, not created it. The rejection parable, which of itself does not lend itself to a polemic in favor of a Samaritan mission, did not originate with him; 9. 51 constitutes the introduction Luke added to the story as he found it. [3] The passage of the healing of the lepers one of whom was a Samaritan is likewise pre-Lucan, though v. 19b ἡ πίστις σου σέσωκέν σε stems from the evangelist, [4] and is his way of underlining that Jesus' attitude towards the Samaritan was not different from his attitude towards Jews, the

[1] e.g. the 13. 31 ff. passage, where Jesus is warned that Antipas wishes to kill him; further 13. 10, where in the Galilean pattern (cf. Mk. 1. 21) he teaches in a synagogue on the Sabbath; further 10. 13 ff., 11. 14 ff. (cf. Mk. 3. 22 ff.), 11. 37 ff. (cf. Mk. 8. 15), 12. 33 ff. (cf. Mk. 6. 19 ff.).

[2] This three-fold scheme is reinforced by the fact that in 17. 11 f. Jesus is still, according to Luke, in Samaria, despite the fact that some of the preceding material is Judean in origin, i.e. 10. 28-37, 10. 38-42, 13. 1-5, 13. 34 f.

[3] ἐγένετο . . . ἐν τῷ . . . . in that verse is typically Lucan, and Luke derived αὐτὸς τὸ πρόσωπον . . . τοῦ πορεύεσθαι εἰς Ἰερουσαλήμ from v. 53. Dibelius, *From Tradition to Gospel*, p. 47, postulates further that the messengers in v. 52 were added by Luke, and he may be right.

[4] So correctly Bultmann, *op. cit.*, p. 33. It is true that Mark brings the phrase ἡ πίστις σου σέσωκέν σε twice, in both of which cases Luke follows him. But the fact that Luke brings the phrase independently twice (here and in 7. 50), and the fact that πίστις is found twenty-seven times in Luke-Acts, whereas it occurs only five times in Mark and seven in Matthew, points conclusively to its having originated here with Luke. V. 11 may also stem from the evangelist, who thus fitted the story about a Samaritan into a scheme of a trip through Samaria, but we cannot be sure on the point. Creed, *op. cit., ad loc.*, postulates that the mention of Samaria at the story's beginning pre-dates the identification of one of the lepers as a Samaritan, and explains how the latter identification came into being. But this is certainly incorrect; if anything, the opposite is true, i. e. the reference to Samaria at the story's beginning was added in order to explain the presence of the Samaritan among the lepers. It is, however, quite likely that both the reference to Jesus' being in Samaria and to one of the lepers being a Samaritan belonged to the account from the beginning.

phrase carrying in addition the theological overtone that, as regards Jesus' saving power, a Samaritan was at no disadvantage as over aginst Jews. [1] As for the story of the good Samaritan, it is one of the parables which we may say with certainty go back to Jesus.

John presents a picture definitely similar, despite the difference in the details; Jesus in ch. 4 journeys through Samaria, engages in a long discourse with a Samaritan woman, and encounters faith among the Samaritans (v. 41 f.). Recently Oscar Cullmann [2] has offered the opinion that the difficult verse 4. 39 refers to the Samaritan mission described in Acts 8, where the Hellenists, represented by Philip, convert the Samaritans, and the apostles (Peter and John) lay hands on them, whereupon they receive the Holy Spirit. This provides an interpretation of v. 38 fitting in well with the reference to the Samaritan (perhaps too, by extension, the Gentile) mission in v. 35; further, it is in harmony with the fact that in John the period and problems of the Church are dealt with exclusively in connection with Jesus' life, whereas in Luke, because of the existence of Acts, this is not the case. John 4, then, in a fashion strikingly similar to the Samaritan material in Luke, points ahead to the Church's Samaritan mission and provides a sanction for it.

How much of John 4 stems from the evangelist? That is a question not easily answered. That much of it does is certain—e.g. the water theme in vv. 10-15, as the double meaning of water and the woman's failure to grasp the true meaning show. Bultmann [3] attributes further vv. 31-39, 41 f. to the evangelist; certainly he is right as regards v. 38, [4] very likely also right as regards the

---

[1] The verse, that is to say, carries the implication that the Samaritan's healing has not only physical but theological consequences (i.e. in the realm of forgiveness); cf. the use of the phrase ἡ πίστις σου σέσωκέν σε elsewhere in Luke: in 7. 50, where it represents an emphasizing of the fact that the sins of the woman who has anointed Jesus have been forgiven; in 8. 48, where its use (in connection with the woman with the issue of blood) is exactly analogous to what it is in 17. 19; and 18. 42, where the words accompany, and perhaps effect, Jesus' healing of Bartimaeus.

[2] In "Samaria and the Origins of the Christian Mission" in *The Early Church*, p. 190. See further Cullmann's "Secte de Qumran, Hellenistes des Actes et Quatriéme Evangile," *Les Manuscrits de la Mer Morte* (Strasburg colloquium May 25-27, 1955), pp. 68 f.

[3] Bultmann, *Evangelium des Johannes, ad loc.*

[4] That this view of v. 38 is shared by Cullmann is clear from his discussion of that verse in "L'opposition contra le Temple de Jérusalem: motif commune de la theologie johannique et du monde ambiant."

notice about the faith of the Samaritans in vv. 41 f. It is not, of course, inconceivable that John created the entire scene of Jesus and the Samaritan woman:[1] but this is to fail to take into account the possibility of John's use of a written or—here more likely—an oral source, and Bultmann[2] is in all likelihood right that the core of ch. 4 was taken over by John.[3] That this core did not consist of the material on Jesus vis-à-vis the Samaritans which John found in Luke's gospel is clear from the degree to which John differs from Luke at this point.[4]

The question must now be asked whether these stories of Jesus' contact with the Samaritans have a historical basis. If Mt. 10. 5 f. ("These twelve Jesus sent out, charging them, 'Go nowhere among the Gentiles, and enter no town of the Samaritans, but go rather to the lost sheep of the house of Israel' ") be accepted as a word of Jesus, they do not. But, on the basis of what we know about him, it

---

[1] So Gardner-Smith, *op. cit.*, p. 20, who sees the evangelist as having done so to provide an anticipation of the Church's Samaritan mission.

[2] Bultmann, *op. cit.*, *ad loc.*

[3] This is confirmed by the fact that, elsewhere in the gospel, in 3. 23, in the note that John baptized near Ainon in Salem (which Kraeling, *op. cit.*, pp. 8 f., correctly calls historical) John gives evidence of a knowledge of traditions about events occurring on Samaritan soil. John Bowman, "Samaritan Studies," *Bulletin of the John Rylands Library* March 1959, pp. 300 ff., goes beyond this and attempts to demonstrate that an extensive relatedness exists between the theology of the fourth gospel and that of the Samaritans. His chief argument concerns the fact that there are signs that in both Johannine and Samaritan thought the messiah was expected as "the prophet" (similar to Moses—cf. Dt. 18. 15 ff.) —e. g. in John, 6. 40, 7. 40-43. But the concept of the (coming) prophet is found not only among the Samaritans and in John's gospel, but also in the Qumran texts and the writings of the Damascus community (see on this Cullmann's *Christology*, pp. 19-22); the argument primarily on this basis of a close connection between Samaritans and John is not, therefore, a strong one. Certainly Jn. 4—e. g. v. 20—shows a knowledge of Samaritan customs; further, as Bowman, p. 313, points out, the title σωτὴρ τοῦ κόσμου in 4. 42 never elsewhere appears in John, but does in Samaritan descriptions of the messiah. But to see John as attempting, in his theology throughout the gospel, to "make a bridge between Samaritans and Jews in Christ" (Bowman, p. 302) is unjustified.

[4] Bacon, *The Fourth Gospel in Research and Debate*, p. 367 maintains that ch. 4 is John's creation, whereby he has combined the Marcan incident of the Syro-Phoenician woman and the Lucan account of Jesus' activity among Samaritans. This is in accord with Bacon's theory that all John's special material is to be explained as the result of the evangelist's combination of Marcan and Lucan material. This theory here as elsewhere is too mechanical; here it fails to account adequately for the great difference between the portrait of the Samaritan women in John and that of the Syro-Phoenician woman in Mark.

is hard to see this statement in its exclusiveness as stemming from the man who, for instance, recounted the parable of the good Samaritan; [1] rather we have in Mt. 10. 5 an early polemic produced by a Jewish-Christian community opposed to the Church's missionary activity among the Samaritans. Even if, with Schniewind, [2] one sees Jesus' word in Mt. 8. 11 (" I tell you, many will come from east and west and sit at table with Abraham, Isaac, and Jesus in the kingdom of heaven . . . . ") as pointing to the conclusion that Jesus thought that the inclusion of the Gentiles in the kingdom would occur only at the end of history, that in no way proves that Mt. 10. 5b, in its negativeness, is genuine; indeed, properly speaking Mt. 8. 11 does not apply to the Samaritans, who did not have to come from east and west, i.e. from the ends of the world. It is true that in Mark Jesus goes from Judea to Galilee not via Samaria but via Trans-Jordan; but Mark's geography in chs. 6-9 is too chaotic for us to be able to attribute to him complete authority in this regard; [3] after all, the directest route between Galilee and Jerusalem lies through Samaria. Even if Jesus once made the trip via Trans-Jordan, it is unlikely that he went from Galilee to Jerusalem only once, [4] or that he always avoided the direct route. Furthermore, the only half-way conceivable hypothesis on the basis of which the creation of Lk. 9. 51-56 by the Church can be postulated [5] is that it arose as a polemic against the Samaritan mission, Jesus' rejection by the Samaritans being devised in order thereby to demonstrate that missionary activity among the Samaritans must be against God's will. But this is very far-fetched; it is preferable to see the passage, with the possible exception of vv. 54 f., as historically accurate. [6] Also, the account of the healing of the lepers in Luke accords well with the picture of Jesus as not seeking out Samaritans—that he did not seek out any non-Jews is clear from the story of the Syro-Phoenician woman (Mk. 7. 24-30)—but at the same time not rigorously avoiding

[1] This should be stressed in opposition to Schniewind, *Das Evangelium nach Matthäus*, *ad loc.*

[2] Schniewind, *op. cit.*, *ad loc.*

[3] See on this p. 108, nt. 1.

[4] See on this pp. 27 f.

[5] Creed, *op. cit.*, *ad loc.*, postulates that we have here an ideal scene originating in the Gentile Church—but that doesn't account for the element the rejection plays in the account.

[6] So K. L. Schmidt, *op. cit.*, p. 267, and Hirsch, *op. cit.*, II, 207—versus Bultmann, *Die Geschichte der synoptischen Tradition*, pp. 24, 57.

them, and willing to go through territory where some were to be found.[1] It further fits well with the picture, confirmed by such stories as that of the Syro-Phoenician woman and the centurion with the sick servant, that Jesus on a number of occasions encountered a more positive response from non-Jews than from Jews—analogous to his experience with tax-collectors and "sinners" as over against Pharisees.

If the verdict as regards the historicity of the two Lucan passages where Jesus comes into contact with Samaritans is positive, that concerning Jn. 4 is less so. The picture given in 4. 41 f., and stemming as we saw from the evangelist, is not historical, involving as it does a real ministry of Jesus among the Samaritans. Furthermore, if it is clear that Jesus in his ministry did not seek out Samaritans, did not consciously take the initiative with them as he did with Jews, then it follows that Jesus did not behave to a Samaritan woman in the way John records. Furthermore, as we've seen, the very details about the water which characterize the relation of Jesus and the woman stem from John; if, as we surmised, a pre-Johannine core lies at the root of the chapter, it did not contain these details. What it contained beyond the bare fact of an encounter of Jesus with a Samaritan woman near the well of Jacob in Samaria we cannot determine. But that this fact is historical we have no reason to doubt.

Have we, in Luke's and John's parallel but independent traditions concerning Jesus and Samaritans, an indication as to where the two evangelists encountered those traditions common to them both, written and oral, which cannot be explained on the basis of

---

[1] Both Luke and John omit Mark's account of Jesus' journey into predominantly Gentile (non-Samaritan) areas, Mk. 7. 24-8. 26. Luke brings pericopes (in 9. 18-43) which in Mark belong to this journey, but in Luke, due to the omission of mention of Caesarea-Philippi in v. 18, do not; John has nothing whatever of this. As has often been pointed out, the historical foundation of this Marcan journey is shaky; the only passage in it whose *contents* label it as possibly non-Galilean is that concerning the Syro-Phoenician woman (7. 24-30)—and even there it is quite possible that the woman was living in Galilee when she sought Jesus out. Furthermore, the journey as described entails an unlikely, circuitous sequence of stops. At most we have here a vague tradition of activity of Jesus among the Gentiles; quite possibly Mark for theological purposes has constructed the whole on the basis of the 7. 24-30 passage alone. That Luke and John didn't bring the journey may have to do with the contents (unacceptable to them) of 7. 24-30; at any rate, for them, Jesus' only activity outside of purely Jewish territory occurred in Samaria.

John's having known the third gospel—i.e. the tradition of the people's having wondered who the Baptist was, of the approach to Jerusalem, of the events (including the footwashing) of the last supper, the hearing before Annas, the charge against Jesus that he claimed to be king, the two disciples' going to the grave and the words the risen Christ speaks to Peter? Did Luke and John encounter these traditions in Samaria, and did John encounter Luke's gospel there? The evidence is against these suppositions. It is true that both evangelists saw in Jesus' contacts with Samaritans an anticipation, and also a justification, of the Church's mission to the Samaritans—which means that both knew of and were in favor of the latter. That does not, however, mean that both evangelists had been to Samaria, for news of the Church's mission there, its first among non-Jews, would have circulated among Christians everywhere. And indeed a large number of factors point to the geographical area of contact as being not Samaria but Jerusalem. In the first place, and most important, all the traditions enumerated above, except that of the miraculous catch, concern events occurring in or near Jerusalem—as do the Martha-Mary cycle of traditions upon which both Luke and John drew. Also, the Samaritan traditions in Luke are traditions which focus on Samaria from a Jerusalem point of view. This is clear for 17. 11-19 from the mention of priests in v. 14; furthermore, it is likely that the tradition of Jesus' rejection in Samaria was preserved in Jerusalem, for such a story was hardly likely to have been treasured by Samaritan Christians.

The strength of this evidence is increased by the fact that both the third and fourth gospels are in their general structure oriented towards Jerusalem. This is seen most clearly as regards the traditions of the resurrection appearances. It is evident also in the geographical scheme of both gospels. Luke by putting in 9. 51 the notice that Jesus turned his face in the direction of Jerusalem, [1] and by reinforcing it with the 13. 22 and 17. 11 notes, has made the whole journey one towards Jerusalem; this fact is of as much importance as the fact that the whole journey is, implicitly, one through Samaria. The result is that the Galilean section, despite the

[1] Mark brings no corresponding notice; though in 10. 1 he says Jesus came into Judea and Transjordan, the notion of a journey to Jerusalem can be deduced in Mark only on the basis of drawing conclusions for ch. 10 from Jesus' entry into Jerusalem in ch. 11.

fact that many of the passages in the journey section are undoubtedly Galilean in origin, [1] is terminated at 9. 30; from then on, though Samaria plays a rôle, the gospel stands under the sign of Jerusalem, the goal of the journey and the locale of the gospel's concluding section (where Jesus appears to dwell for a longer period of time than in Mark). [2] Furthermore, the first two chapters center about Jerusalem and its temple and about Judea (Bethlehem)—1. 26-38 constitute a brief, necessary Galilean interlude in the Jerusalem-dominated tradition. Galilee as locale is therefore restricted to 4. 14-9. 50, i.e. to less than six of the gospel's twenty-four chapters — whereas in Mark Jesus is in Galilee (or the sea of Galilee area) from 1. 14 to the end of 9, i.e. for more than eight of the gospel's sixteen chapters. [3] In John, after 2. 13, Jesus only once (in ch. 6) is reported to be voluntarily in Galilee—otherwise he goes there (i.e. in ch. 4) only because of the hostility of the Jews in Judea. Before 2. 13 he is in Galilee only in 1. 43-2. 12. Actually, in John, only five traditions, that of the choosing of the disciples, the wedding in Cana, the healing of the courtier's son, the feeding of the five thousand and the controversy with his brothers, tie Jesus to Galilee—though the first and last of these indicate how historically irreproachable the tradition of Jesus' Galilean origin is.

This evidence all points to Jerusalem as the source of the related traditions which Luke and John independently bring—as well as of the most important of the traditions as regards which John follows Luke, i.e. that of Jesus' appearance to the eleven in Jerusalem; and the Samaritan passages point to Jerusalem or ex-Jerusalem circles in which the Church's mission in Samaria was regarded in a favorable light. How, we must now ask, did the traditions which Luke and John offer independently come into the hands of the two evangelists? Assuming that Paul's travel companion Luke, the author of the "we" sections of Acts, also put together the whole of Luke-Acts, [4] then the simplest explanation is that he gathered these traditions in the course of the time he

[1] See above, p. 104, nt. 5. [2] See p. 49 nt. 1.

[3] We do not suggest that Luke derived the geographical scheme of his gospel, directly or indirectly, from a Jerusalem source—for it certainly originated with him. But the very fact that he organized his gospel in such a way shows the rôle Jerusalem played in his thought, which rôle is most easily explained on the basis of his having had, directly or indirectly, contact with Jerusalem—on which see below.

[4] This is the unopposed tradition of the early Church going back to the anti-Marcion Luke prologue, and of the great majority of commentators.

spent with Paul in Jerusalem and Caesarea (Acts 21. 8-18). Though it is possible that some of these traditions may have been transmitted to him from the Jewish-Christian Silas of Jerusalem with whom for a while he travelled (Acts 15. 22-18. 17), it has been suggested that Luke's main source of information was Philip and his daughters in Caesarea (Acts 21. 8 f.), [1] for which support can be found in the fact that Eusebius [2] says that Papias, who had spoken to the daughters, had received traditions from them. According to this view, Philip's traditions originated in Jerusalem and came with him via Samaria to Caesarea. This is an attractive hypothesis, accounting admirably for the material in the third gospel and in Acts dealing with Samaria. Also, the fact that a number of the traditions Luke has in common with John came to him in written form [3] constitutes no problem for this hypothesis; in all likelihood these passages had been written down for catechetical or liturgical purposes, and no one would have been more likely to possess such than a missionary like Philip.

As far as John is concerned, the picture of his having gathered in Jerusalem the traditions he shares with but did not find in Luke, fits well with the generally accepted critical view which holds that the fourth evangelist knew Jerusalem at first hand, as his knowledge, for example, of the festivals in Jerusalem indicates; this view has been confirmed by the parallels between Johannine material and that in the Dead Sea scrolls. [4] Recently Cullmann, [5] pointing

It is not necessary here to review the many arguments which can be advanced in support of this view as well as the difficulties confronting it. Suffice it to say that (a) everyone grants that there is stylistic uniformity between the "we" sections and the rest of Acts; (b) this means that the same hand was responsible for the final version of all sections of Acts (and of the third gospel;) (c) this hand must have been that of the original author of the "we" sections, because if a later writer had rewritten the "we" sections in the course of incorporating them into his account (that in this case he would have had to rewrite them is clear from the stylistic uniformity between these sections and the rest of Acts) he would certainly have removed all traces of the first person plural.

[1] So Harnack, *Luke the Physician*, p. 124, Streeter, *Oxford Studies in the Synoptic Problem*, p. 224, Bartlet, *ibid.*, pp. 351 ff., and Sanday, *ibid.*, p. xxi.

[2] *Historia ecclesiastica*, III, 39, 3.

[3] i. e. that of the approach to Jerusalem and of the examination before Caiaphas.

[4] For these parallels see K. G. Kuhn, "Die in Palästina gefundenen hebräischen Texte und das Neue Testament," *Zeitschrift für Theologie und Kirche*, 1950, pp. 193 ff.

[5] In "L'opposition contra le Temple de Jérusalem: motif commune de la theologie johannique et du monde ambiant."

to the opposition to the temple found both in John (e.g. 4. 21) and in the speech of the Hellenist Stephen (Acts 7, e.g. v. 48), has advanced the interesting opinion that the fourth evangelist, an ex-disciple of John the Baptist, was a Hellenist, of the same party as Stephen and Philip. This explains very well the knowledge of an interest in Judea and Jerusalem manifest in the fourth gospel, the interest in Samaria, and the overlapping of Johannine and Lucan traditions. Furthermore, for the fourth evangelist's having had direct access to Jerusalem traditions which Luke only had at second hand, via Philip, speaks the fact that in at least two cases, that of the approach to Jerusalem and the serving at the last supper, what is clear in John (or, in the case of the fishing miracle, primary in John) is unclear (or secondary) in Luke.

It's been suggested [1] that Philip the evangelist of Acts 6, 8 and 21 is to be identified with Philip, a disciple of Jesus, about whom the fourth gospel (in 1. 44 ff., 6. 5 ff., 12. 21 f. and 14. 9 f.) brings a number of traditions not found in the other gospels. For this view speaks the notice in Jn. 12. 20 f. that this Philip served as an intermediary between certain men of non-Jewish birth [2] and Jesus—so also the fact that Philip as described in Acts belongs to the same, Hellenist circle of which the fourth evangelist was probably a member. But this equation is not without its difficulties. According to the synoptic tradition one of the twelve was named Philip, but this was clearly not the man later known as Philip the evangelist; Luke, who as we saw probably personally knew Philip the evangelist, in Acts 6. 6 specifically distinguishes him, as one of the deacons, from the twelve. This makes it difficult to identify him with the fourth evangelist's Philip, except on the assumption that the latter also was not reckoned as one of the twelve, even though he had been a follower of Jesus in his lifetime. But this assumption involves the supposition that two among Jesus' immediate followers (Philip one of the twelve and Philip later known as the evangelist) were named Philip, which considering that it is a Greek name, is exceedingly unlikely; further, the question raises itself in that case why Luke, knowing so much about Philip the evangelist, didn't mention the fact that he'd been a disciple of Jesus. The difficulties

[1] By e. g. Zurhellen, *op. cit.*, p. 55 and Gardner-Smith, *op. cit.*, p. 18.

[2] That Ἕλληνες means this, and not specifically Greeks, is clear from Jn. 7. 25 as well as from Mk. 7. 26, as Barrett, *op. cit.*, *ad loc.*, correctly points out.

here are too great; the hypothesis simply cannot be maintained. [1]

Two questions remain to be answered, that of where and when John encountered Luke's gospel. It is difficult to find the answer to the first of these questions due to the fact that we don't know where Luke's gospel was written [2]—whether in Achaia [3] or Rome [4] or Ephesus. [5] Even if the traditions connecting John's gospel to Ephesus be accepted, [6] it can't be assumed that John encountered Luke's gospel there, for we don't know how long the fourth evangelist remained in Palestine, whether he went straight to Ephesus (or first stayed a while in Samaria?), and was there by the time Luke was written. It is better to admit that we do not know the answer to this question than to guess. As to the question when

---

[1] One other critical opinion must be mentioned. Harnack, *op. cit.*, p. 108, thinks that the traditions Luke and John bring independently were carried from Jerusalem by Christians emigrating from Palestine, at the time of the siege or afterwards, and were thus encountered by both Luke and John somewhere outside Palestine—and Zurhellen, *op. cit.*, pp. 62 f., suggests that Antioch was the place. But, as we've seen, there is no need to postulate that either Luke or John found these traditions elsewhere than in Palestine. Harnack, *ibid.*, asks why, if Luke and John found these traditions in Palestine, they weren't known to and offered by the Palestinian Mark? As a matter of fact, Mark probably knew the Lucan-Johannine traditions in seven cases where these appear to be historical, and his failure to use them in no case presents a problem. The seven are the people's asking who the Baptist was, the account of the approach to Jerusalem which presupposed that Jesus had been there before, the footwashing at the last supper, the chronology of the last supper events, the accusation that Jesus claimed to be king, the visit of the two disciples to the tomb and the resurrection appearance to Peter. As for the second, Mark could not use it for the reason that according to his gospel Jesus had not previously been to Jerusalem. As for the third and fourth, Mark suppressed them in order to produce a less problematical account of the last supper, and one dominated by the institution of the Lord's Supper. As for the sixth and seventh, Mark, terminating his gospel immediately after the angel appeared to the women at the tomb, had no place for them. As to the first and fifth, Mark's failure to use them was merely accidental.

[2] So, correctly, Feine-Behm, *op. cit.*, p. 90, and Goguel, *Introduction au Nouveau Testament*, I, p. 526.

[3] So the anti-Marcion Lucan prologue.

[4] So Michaelis, *Einleitung in das Neue Testament*, p. 78.

[5] So Goodspeed, *Introduction to the New Testament*, p. 208.

[6] For the evidence against these traditions see Zurhellen, *op. cit.*, pp. 34 ff. Zurhellen, *ibid*, pp. 61 ff., attempts to demonstrate that John's gospel was written not in Ephesus but in Antioch. However, insofar as this attempt is bound up with his view that Antioch is the source of the common Luke-John traditions, it cannot stand. Even if, as is possible, the evangelist wrote the fourth gospel in Antioch, he did not gather his material there—that came with him from Palestine.

John encountered Luke's gospel, we know that he did so before he wrote his own gospel. As a matter of fact, the date of the writing of the third gospel provides the *terminus a quo* for the writing of the fourth gospel. When did Luke write his gospel? A comparison of Lk. 21. 20 ff. with the corresponding verses of Mk. 13 shows that Luke wrote after the siege of Jerusalem; [1] we can say further that 74, as the date of the earliest empire-wide census, is the earliest possible date for Luke's composition, [2] and the late 70's are probably a reasonable estimate as to when Luke wrote his gospel. [3] Very soon after that, around 80, we may safely postulate that John encountered Luke's gospel, which encounter, compounded as it was of both positive and negative reactions, was one of the decisive factors crystallizing in John's mind a picture of what a gospel should be and stimulating him, in the next several years, to write his own gospel.

---

[1] So the majority of critics, e.g. Creed, *op. cit.*, xxii, and Haenchen, *op. cit.*, p. 105.

[2] So Joachim Jeremias, *Die Abendmahlsworte*, 1st. ed., p. 46, nt. 1.

[3] Goguel, *op. cit.*, p. 527, says 75-80.

SUMMARY

Our examination of the traditions common to Luke's and John's gospels is completed. We have seen that John knew Luke's gospel, and that he drew on Luke for elements in his account of the anointing of Jesus, of the last supper and last discourse, of the high-priestly prayer, of the arrest, of the trial before Pilate, of the crucifixion, death and burial, and of the appearances of Jesus in Jerusalem. Not all the similarities between Luke and John are, however, to be so explained. At a large number of points—as regards the people's wondering who the Baptist was, the fishing miracle, the approach to Jerusalem, Jesus' serving at the last supper and the chronology of the events there, the hearing before Annas, the charge against Jesus that he claimed to be king, the two disciples' going to the grave and the words the risen Christ speaks to Peter—Luke and John bring traditions which, though related, came independently to the two of them. The means by which this happened vary—e.g. in the case of the approach to Jerusalem the two evangelists drew on similar, but not identical, written accounts of the event, whereas they both knew the same oral account of the last supper and the same written account of Jesus' examination before Annas. What characterizes the instances of related material is, indeed, the variety of the means by which the relationship came about; there is no evidence for either Luke's or John's having drawn such material from a continuous source which one or both of them knew. Rather the evidence of our analysis points to the existence in the Church at the time both evangelists wrote of many isolated written and oral traditions—the former having been written down in connection with their use for catechetical or liturgical purposes—on which (in addition to Mark) the two writers drew. In this regard our investigation has confirmed the validity of the assertions of the form-critics, indicating in addition that the period in which isolated stories circulated as such was a long one, extending over a period of at least fifty years after the resurrection. We saw, further, that the evidence points to virtually all of the traditions coming independently to Luke and John as having originated in Jerusalem—John having found them there and Luke, probably, finding them in Caesarea. Finally, the verdict as to the historicity of these common traditions varied from case to case but it was, on the whole, a markedly favorable one—one which should serve as a check to those critics who, at the expense of Luke and even more of John, regard Mark as *the* historical gospel.

BIBLIOGRAPHY

ALBERTZ, Martin, *Die Botschaft des Neuen Testamentes*, I/1. Zürich, 1947.
ALBRIGHT, W. F., "Recent Discoveries in Palestine and the Gospel of John," *The Background of the New Testament and its Eschatology*, ed. W. D. Davies and D. Daube. Cambridge, England, 1956.
D'AYGALLIERS, A. WAUTIER, *Les Sources du Recit de la Passion chez Luc.* Alençon, 1920.
BACON, B. W., *The Fourth Gospel in Research and Debate.* London, 1910.
BAUER, Walter, *Das Johannesevangelium.* Tübingen, 1933.
——, *Das Leben Jesu im Zeitalter der neutestamentlichen Apokryphen.* Tübingen, 1910.
——, *Wörterbuch zum Neuen Testament*, 5th ed. Berlin, 1958.
BAYER, H. W., διακονέω in *Theologisches Wörterbuch zum Neuen Testament*, ed. G. Kittel, II. Stuttgart, 1933.
BERNARD, J. H., *Gospel According to St. John*, Edinburgh, 1928.
BERTRAM, G., *Die Leidensgeschichte Jesu und der Christuskult.* Göttingen, 1922.
BICKERMANN, E., "Utilitas Crucis," *Revue de l'Histoire des Religions.* Paris, 1935.
BLACK, Matthew, *An Aramaic Approach to the Gospels and Acts.* Oxford, 1946.
BLASS, F. and DEBRUNNER, A., *Grammatik des neutestamentlichen Griechisch.* Göttingen, 1949.
BOWMAN, John, "Samaritan Studies," *Bulletin of the John Rylands Library.* Manchester, March, 1958.
BRUCE, F. F., *The Acts of the Apostles*, London, 1951.
BULTMANN, R., *Das Evangelium des Johannes.* Göttingen, 1941.
——, *Die Geschichte der synoptischen Tradition*, 3rd ed. Göttingen, 1957.
——, "Zur johanneischen Tradition," *Theologische Literaturzeitung*, Leipzig, 1957.
Burkitt, F. C., *Christian Beginnings.* London, 1924.
BUSSMANN, Wilhelm. *Synoptische Studien*, III. Halle, 1931.
CADBURY, H. F., *The Making of Luke-Acts.* London, 1927.
v. CAMPENHAUSEN, Hans, *Der Ablauf der Osterereignisse und das Leere Grab.* Heidelberg, 1952.
CLEMEN, Carl, *Die Entstehung des Johannesevangeliums.* Halle, 1912.
CONZELMANN, Hans, *Die Mitte der Zeit.* Tübingen, 1954.
CREED, J. M., *The Gospel according to St. Luke*, London, 1924.
CULLMANN, Oscar, *The Christology of the New Testament*, trans. S. C. Guthrie and C. A. M. Hall. Philadelphia, 1959.
——, "L'opposition contra le Temple de Jerusalem: motif commune de la theologie johannique et du monde ambiant," paper read in September 1958 at the meeting of the Society of New Testament Studies in Strasbourg.
——, *Peter*, trans. F. V. Filson. London, 1953.
——, Πέτρος, Κηφᾶς in *Theologisches Wörterbuch zum Neuen Testament*, ed. G. Kittel, VI. Stuttgart.
——, "Samaria and the Origins of the Christian Mission," *The Early Church.* London, 1956.

——, "Secte de Qumran, Hellenistes des Actes et Quatrième Evangile," *Les Manuscrits de la Mer Morte* (Strasbourg colloquium May 25-27 1955). Paris, 1957.

——, "The Significance of the Qumran Texts for Research into the Beginnings of Christianity" (reprinted from the *Journal of Biblical Literature*, 1955), *The Scrolls and the New Testament*, ed. K. Stendahl. New York, 1957.

——, *The State in the New Testament*. New York, 1956.

——, *Urchristentum und Gottesdienst*. Zürich, 1950.

DALMAN, Gustaf, *Jesus-Jeshua*, trans. P. P. Levertoff. New York, 1929.

DIBELIUS, Martin, "Die alttestamentliche Motive in der Leidensgeschichte des Petrus- und des Johannes-Evangeliums," *Zeitschrift für die Alttestamentliche Wissenschaft*, supplement 33. Giessen, 1918.

——, *From Tradition to Gospel*, trans. B. L. Woolf. London, 1934.

——, "Herodes und Pilatus," *Zeitschrift für die Neutestamentliche Wissenschaft*. Berlin, 1915.

——, "Johannesevangelium," *Die Religion in Geschichte und Gegenwart*, 2nd ed., III. Tübingen, 1929.

——, "Taylor's *Behind the Third Gospel*," *Theologische Literaturzeitung*. Leipzig, 1927.

——, *Die Urchristliche Ueberlieferung von Johannes dem Täufer*. Göttingen, 1911.

EATON, B. S., *The Gospel according to St. Luke*. Edinburgh, 1930.

ERBES, C., "Der Apostel Johannes und der Jünger, welcher an der Brust des Herrn lag," *Zeitschrift für Kirchengeschichte*. Gotha, 1912.

EWALD, Paul, *Das Hauptproblem der Evangelienfrage*. Leipzig, 1890.

FEINE, P. and BEHM, J., *Einleitung in das Neue Testament*, 10th ed. Heidelberg, 1954.

FINEGAN, Jack, *Die Ueberlieferung der Leidens- und Auferstehungsgeschichte*. Giessen, 1934.

GARDNER-SMITH, P., *St. John and the Synoptic Gospels*. Cambridge, 1938.

GAUSSEN, H., "The Lucan and Johannine Writings," *The Journal of Theological Studies*. Oxford, 1908.

GILMOUR, S. MacLean., *The Gospel according to St. Luke: The Interpreter's Bible*, VIII. New York, 1952.

GOGUEL, Maurice, "A propos du procès de Jesus," *Zeitschrift für die Neutestamentliche Wissenschaft*. Berlin, 1932.

——, *Au Seuil de l'Evangile. Jean-Baptiste*. Paris, 1928.

——, *The Birth of Christianity*, trans. H. C. Snape. New York, 1954.

——, *La Foi à la Résurrection de Jésus dans le Christianisme primitif*. Paris, 1933.

——, *Introduction au Nouveau Testament*, I, II. Paris, 1923-4.

——, *The Life of Jesus*, trans. O. Wyon. New York, 1954.

——, *Les Sources du Récit Johannique de la Passion*. La Roche-sur-Yon, 1910.

GOODSPEED, E. J., *Introduction to the New Testament*. Chicago, 1937.

GRANT, F. C., "Was the Author of John dependent upon the Gospel of Luke ?", *Journal of Biblical Literature*. Philadelphia, 1937.

GRASS, Hans, *Ostergeschehen und Osterberichte*. Göttingen, 1956.

GRASSER, Erich, *Das Problem der Parusieverzögerung in den synoptischen Evangelien und in der Apostelgeschichte*. West Berlin, 1957.

GUMBEL, L., *Das Johannes-Evangelium eine Ergänzung des Lukas-Evangeliums*. Speyer, 1908/9.

HAENCHEN, Ernst, "Aus der Literatur zum Johannesevangelium, 1929-1956," *Theologische Rundschau*. Tübingen, 1955.
——, *Die Apostelgeschichte*. Göttingen, 1956.
v. HARNACK, *The Acts of the Apostles*, trans. J. R. Wilkinson. London and New York, 1909.
——, *Luke the Physician*, trans. J. R. Wilkinson. New York, 1908.
HAWKINS, J. C., *Horae Synopticae*. Oxford, 1899.
HIRSCH, E., *Frühgeschichte des Evangeliums*, II. Tübingen, 1941.
HOLTZMANN, H. J., "Das schriftstellerische Verhältnis des Johannes zu den Synoptikern," *Zeitschrift für wissenschaftliche Theologie*. Jena, 1869.
HOSKYNS, E. G., *The Fourth Gospel*, 2nd ed. London, 1948.
——, "Notes and Studies," *Journal of Theological Studies*. Oxford, 1920.
HOWARD, Wilbert F., *The Gospel according to St. Luke: The Interpreter's Bible*, VIII. New York, 1952.
JAUBERT, A., *La Date de la Cène*. Paris, 1957.
JEREMIAS, Joachim, *Die Abendmahlsworte Jesu*, 1st ed. Göttingen, 1935.
——, *The Eucharistic Words of Jesus*, trans. from the 2nd ed. by A. Ehrhardt. New York, 1955.
——, *Jerusalem zur Zeit Jesu*, IIB. Leipzig, 1929.
——, "Pericopen-Umstellungen bei Lukas?", *New Testament Studies*. Cambridge, 1956.
——, "Zur Geschichtlichkeit des Verhörs Jesu vor dem Hohen Rat," *Zeitschrift für die Neutestamentliche Wissenschaft*, Berlin, 1950/1.
JUELICHER, A. and FASCHER, E., *Einleitung in das Neue Testament*. Tübingen, 1931.
KAESEMANN, Ernst, "Ketzer und Zeuge," *Zeitschrift für Theologie und Kirche*. Tübingen, 1951.
KLOSTERMANN, Erich, *Das Lukasevangelium*, 2nd. ed. Tübingen, 1929.
——, *Das Markusevangelium*, Tübingen, 1926.
KRAELING, Carl, *John the Baptist*. New York, 1951.
KUHN, K. G., "Die in Palestina gefundenen hebraischen Texte und das Neue Testament," *Zeitschrift für Theologie und Kirche*. Tübingen, 1950.
LAGRANGE, M. J., *Evangile selon Saint Luc*, 8th ed. Paris, 1948.
LAKE, KIRSOPP and CADBURY, H. J., *The Beginnings of Christianity*, IV. London, 1933.
LARFELD, W., *Die Neutestamentliche Evangelien nach ihrer Eigenart und Abhangigkeit*. Gütersloh, 1925.
LIDDELL and SCOTT, *A Greek-English Lexicon*, 9th ed. revised by Jones and McKenzie. Oxford, 1940.
LIETZMANN, Hans, "Der Prozess Jesu," *Sitzungsbericht der preussischen Akademie der Wissenschaften*. Berlin, 1931.
LIGHTFOOT, R. H., *History and Interpretation in the Gospels*. New York, 1934.
LOHMEYER, Ernst, *Das Urchristentum*, I (*Johannes der Täufer*). Göttingen, 1932.
——, *Das Evangelium des Markus*. Göttingen, 1937.
——, *Galiläa und Jerusalem*. Göttingen, 1936.
LOHSE, Eduard, "Missionarisches Handeln Jesu nach dem Evangelium des Lukas," *Theologische Zeitschrift*. Basel, 1954.
LOISY, Alfred, *Les Actes des Apôtres*. Paris, 1920.
——, *L'Evangile selon Luc*. Paris, 1924.
LUCE, H. K., *The Gospel according to S. Luke*. Cambridge, 1933.
MANSON, William, *The Gospel of Luke*. New York, 1930.
MARXSEN, Willi, *Der Evangelist Markus*. Göttingen, 1956.

MENOUD, Philippe, "Remarques sur les textes de l'ascension dans Luc-Actes," *Neutestamentliche Studien für Rudolf Bultmann*. Berlin, 1954.
MERX, Adalbert, *Das Evangelium des Johannes*. Berlin, 1911.
MICHAELIS, Wilhelm, *Einleitung in das Neue Testament*, 2nd ed. Bern, 1954.
——, *Die Erscheinungen des Auferstandenen*. Basel, 1944.
MORGENTHALER, Robert, *Die lukanische Geschichtschreibung als Zeugnis*, I. Zürich, 1948.
MOWRY, Lucetta, "The Dead Sea Scrolls and the Background for the Gospel of John," *The Biblical Archaeologist*. New Haven, 1954.
OSTY, E., "Les Points de Contact entre le Récit de la Passion dans Saint Luc et Saint Jean," *Mélanges Jules Lebreton, Récherches de Science Religieuse*. Paris, 1951.
OVERBECK, Franz. *Das Johannesevangelium*. Tübingen, 1911.
Oxford Studies in the Synoptic Problem, ed. W. Sanday. Oxford, 1911.
PLUMMER. Alfred. *The Gospel according to S. Luke*, 5th ed. Edinburgh, 1922.
PREISKER, H., "Das Verrat des Judas und das Abendmahl," *Zeitschrift für die Neutestamentliche Wissenschaft*. Berlin, 1942.
REICKE, Bo., *Diakonie, Festfreude und Zelos*. Uppsala, 1951.
——, *Glaube und Leben der Urgemeinde*. Zürich, 1957.
RENGSTORF, K. H., *Das Evangelium nach Lukas*. Göttingen, 1937.
ROHRBACH, Paul, *Die Berichte über die Auferstehung Jesu Christi*. Berlin, 1898.
RUCKSTUHL, Eugen, *Die literarische Einheit des Johannesevangeliums*. Fribourg (Switzerland), 1951.
SCHLATTER, A., *Das Evangelium des Lukas*. Stuttgart, 1931.
——, *Die Sprache und Heimat des vierten Evangelistens*. Gütersloh, 1902.
SCHMID, Josef, *Das Evangelium nach Lukas*. Regensburg, 1955.
SCHMIDT, K. L., *Der Rahmen der Geschichte Jesu*, Berlin, 1919.
SCHNIEWIND, Julius, *Das Evangelium nach Matthäus*. Göttingen, 1937.
——, *Die Parallelperikopen bei Lukas und Johannes*. Leipzig, 1914.
SCHUBERT, Paul, "The Structure and Significance of Luke 24," *Neutestamentliche Studien für Rudolf Bultmann*. Berlin, 1954.
v. SCHUBERT, Hans, *Die Composition des Pseudopetrinischen Evangelienfragments*. Berlin, 1897.
SCHUERER, Emil, *Geschichte des Jüdischen Volkes*, 4th ed. Leipzig, 1901-1909.
SIGGE, Timotheus, *Das Johannesevangelium und die Synoptiker*. Münster, 1935.
SPITTA, Friedrich, *Die Auferstehung Jesu*. Göttingen, 1918.
STRACK, H. L. and BILLERBECK, P., *Kommentar zum Neuen Testament aus Talmud und Midrasch*, II. Munich, 1924.
STRATHMANN, H., *Das Evangelium nach Johannes*. Göttingen, 1951.
STRAUSS, D. F., *The Life of Jesus*, trans. George Eliot. London, 1892.
STREETER, B. H., *The Four Gospels*, 1st ed., 7th impression. London, 1951.
STULCKEN, A., "Petrusevangelium," *Handbuch zu den Neutestamentlichen Apokryphen*, ed. E. Hennecke. Tübingen, 1914.
v. SYBEL, L., "Die Salbungen," *Zeitschrift für die Neutestamentliche Wissenschaft*. Berlin, 1924.
TAYLOR, Vincent, *Behind the Third Gospel*. Oxford, 1926.
——, *The Formation of the Gospel Tradition*. London, 1949.
——, *The Gospel according to St. Mark*. London, 1952.
——, "The Proto-Luke Hypothesis," *Expository Times*. Edinburgh, 1955.
WEISS, Bernhard, *Die Evangelien des Markus und Lukas*, 9th ed. Göttingen, 1901.

WEISS, Bernhard, *Quellen des Lukasevangeliums*. Stuttgart, 1907.
WELLHAUSEN, J., *Einleitung in die drei ersten Evangelien*, 2nd ed. Berlin, 1911.
——, *Das Evangelium Johannis*. Berlin, 1908.
——, *Das Evangelium Lucae*. Berlin, 1904.
WERNLE, P., *Die Synoptische Frage*. Freiburg (Germany), 1899.
WIKENHAUSER, A., *Die Apostelgeschichte*. Regensburg, 1956.
——, *Johannes*. Regensburg, 1957.
WINDISCH, H., *Johannes und die Synoptiker*. Leipzig, 1926.
WUTTIG, O., *Das Johanneische Evangelium und seine Abfassungszeit*. Leipzig, 1897.
ZAHN, Theodor, *Das Evangelium des Lucas*. Leipzig, 1913.
ZIMMERMANN, H., "Lukas und die johanneische Tradition," *Studien und Kritiken*. Gotha, 1913.
ZÖCKLER, O., *Das Kreuz Christi*. Gütersloh, 1875.
ZURHELLEN, O., *Die Heimat des vierten Evangeliums*. Tübingen, 1909.